12/04

MORNING GLORY

The Sonrise Farm Series Book 4

Other books by Katy Pistole

The Palomino
Stolen Gold
Flying High

KATY PISTOLE

MORNING GLORY

THE SONRISE FARM SERIES

BOOK • FOUR

Pacific Press® Publishing Association
Nampa, Idaho
Oshawa, Ontario, Canada
www.pacificpress.com

Designed by Dennis Ferree
Cover art © by Douglas C. Klauba

Copyright © 2004 by
Pacific Press® Publishing Association
Printed in United States of America

Additional copies of this book are available by calling toll free
1-800-765-6955 or by visiting <http://www.adventistbookcenter.com>

ISBN: 0-8163-2036-5

04 05 06 07 08 • 5 4 3 2 1

Dedication

To Jan Smith and Ruth Hudock.
You are true friends and sisters in Him.
I love you both.

In memory of
my sweet friend Beverly Ruybalid
March 1, 1960–November 21, 2003

"Therefore, if anyone is in Christ, he is a new
creation; the old has gone, the new has come!"
(2 Corinthians 5:17, NIV).

Acknowledgments

Thank you to my dear friends, Jan Smith and Ruth Hudock. You helped me more than you will ever know. You are my editors and loving critics.

To Pat and Linda Parelli, John Lyons, Monty Roberts, Nita Jo Rush, Gina Torrell, and all the other wonderful folks working tirelessly to make horses' lives better.

To Dr. Robert Miller, for his work on foal imprinting and proprioception. To my horses, who teach me and remind me constantly of the passionate love my Lord has for me.

And finally, to my Savior Jesus Christ. Your amazing love constantly surprises and awes me. It is all about You. Everything, everywhere.

Contents

Chapter One

The big palomino mare whickered anxiously, kicking at her hugely pregnant belly. Her floor-length, platinum-colored tail flashed back and forth, sending pine shavings in all directions.

Jenny Thomas, sleeping on a cot just outside the stall, was awakened by the rustling sounds. "Sunny?" she called out drowsily, glancing at the clock high on the white, sterile wall of the equine hospital. *Three o'clock in the morning. Is this the moment I've been waiting for?* she wondered, feeling the veil of exhaustion begin to drift slowly back over her. Sleep felt comfortable, like a heavy old blanket. *Two weeks of foal watch. How much more can I take?* she thought.

Jenny forced herself up to a standing position, pressing her cheek against the cool stall door, her sleepy mind wandering. Jenny's heart took inventory of the last year and a half. *Let's see. I lost Sunny, got her back, broke the world record in the puissance, moved to Sonrise Farm. Discovered Sunny's pregnancy. Now here at Equine General Hospital, waiting for this foal. Never dull,* she realized, smiling to herself.

She gazed at Sunny. *Beloved Sunny.*

"What's wrong, Sunny girl? Just restless?"

The mare turned her large, soft eyes on Jenny for a moment then tucked her tail and flopped down onto her side in the soft bedding of the huge foaling stall. Two little gray hooves were poking out from under the mare's tail.

Yes! It's time . . . finally! Exhaustion evaporated as her adrenaline kicked in.

Jenny slid the stall door open, slapping the emergency call buzzer on her way into the stall. She knelt next to Sunny's head and stroked the mare's face. "Help is on the way, girl," she crooned softly. *I'm sure glad we're at a hospital.*

The mare groaned and strained. Jenny watched Sunny's abdominal muscles harden as a contraction took control of the mare's body. Jenny shuffled tailward on her knees to see if any more of the foal had emerged. *Still two hooves.*

Sunny sucked in a deep breath and lifted her head off the floor. A couple more contractions occurred. Jenny kept a close watch on Sunny's tail end. *No progress.*

"Where is everybody?" Jenny muttered, looking around. The foaling wing of the hospital was deserted. *Maybe I should buzz the front desk again,* she thought, staring at the red buzzer. Panic began to rise. She felt it build and threaten to take control. "Lord, help us," Jenny cried out.

The contraction ended. Sunny's nostrils flared as she prepared for the next one. Moments passed before the next mammoth contraction started. *Still just the feet. Are they back feet or front feet?* The thought of a breech[1] foaling sent a flash of fear through Jenny's body. She jumped up and pounded the red emergency buzzer over and over. She peered at the security camera in the far corner. The green light wasn't blinking. *The camera is broken!* she realized with horror. *Why isn't anyone coming?*

Sunny's quiet moan brought Jenny back down to the floor. She glanced at the clock on the wall. *Three twenty-seven. We should be further along by now, Sunny.* "Please, Lord," Jenny begged out loud. "Keep her alive."

I am the Lord of life and death, He gently reminded her. **I am able.**

Jenny noticed that only two feet were showing still. She returned to Sunny's head. The mare seemed unaware of anything except the huge struggle going on within her. Jenny stroked the mare's gold neck.

"I need to get help, Sunny," she whispered through her tears. "Something is terribly wrong. I'll be right back."

Jenny stood up for a mad dash to the front desk at the same time a vet technician sauntered through the swinging doors, arms loaded with laundry.

"Paul!" Jenny's relief flooded her. "Sunny's in trouble. The foal won't come."

Paul nodded and disappeared back through the doors.

"Help is on the way now," Jenny breathed.

After three minutes, which seemed like hours to Jenny, Dr. Andrews strode through the doors.

"What's happening, Jen?" he inquired urgently. "How long has she been down?"

"She went down around three, so it's been about thirty minutes." Jenny sniffled after a quick look at the clock on the wall. "She's been pushing and pushing, but all I see are two little feet."

"All right, Sunny, let's see what's going on here," Dr. Andrews said softly, dropping down on all fours. Sunny groaned as another contraction began.

Dr. Andrews looked worried as he examined Sunny. "Well, Jen, here's the problem. The foal's head is caught under the foreleg. I'm going to have to reposition this foal. And I need help. Where is everyone?" Dr. Andrews demanded, glancing around the empty hallway.

"It's been deserted all night," Jenny said with a shrug.

"Then I guess it's you and me, Jenny. I'm going to have a chat with my night technicians later. You stay at her head and keep her flat. I don't want her trying to get up halfway through. Sit on her head if you need to."

"I won't need to," Jenny replied.

"I need to push this monster back a little," he grunted. "Good grief, this foal is *huge!*" Jenny could hear the physical strain as he panted and pushed. The vet stopped for a second to catch his breath. "Come on, Sunny," Dr. Andrews pleaded. "Stop pushing so hard. I'm trying to help you." He tried yet another position but without success. "We may have to anesthetize her, Jen," the veterinarian said grimly. "These contractions are going to break my arm *and* crush the foal."

Jenny could only rub Sunny's face helplessly.

Sing to her.

"You are my sunshine, my only sunshine. You make me happy, when skies are gray," she sang softly.

The mare's ears swiveled around as she listened to Jenny's voice.

Lord, please make her stop pushing for a minute.

"That's better," the vet said. "Now if I could just lift the nose up and . . . ah, there we go." Dr. Andrews grimaced. "I've got it. We're unstuck." He sat back against the wall, peeling off his long glove. "Now it's up to her."

Sunny gave a huge push. A muzzle slid forth. Then water, water everywhere, and the foal's shoulders slipped out. Dr. Andrews poked his finger into the thick gray birth sac to peel it away from the foal's face. Jenny saw the pale gold hide and paler forelock.

Another palomino, she cheered silently, scooting back to see the baby. She and the vet waited quietly as the foal inched its way out into the world.

"Looks like a filly, Jen," Dr. Andrews announced, placing the baby right in front of Jenny. "And she's gorgeous."

Jenny began rubbing the filly with a fluffy white towel from her foal imprinting kit. The baby shook her head like a drunken dog after a bath. She blinked painfully in the bright light, and her head seemed too heavy for her neck. Long ears, longer legs.

Sunny's baby! A golden filly. Jenny felt her heart swell and engulf the foal.

"Sunny!" Jenny cried, pulling the foal into her lap. "Your baby is here, and she's beautiful."

Sunny didn't move.

---

[1] In a breech birth, the hind feet or buttocks appear first.

Chapter Two

Dr. Andrews leapt up, pulling his stethoscope from his neck. He checked Sunny's heart rate and eye reflex.

"She's going into shock," he exclaimed. "Her color is terrible. I don't know what happened, but we may be losing her. Help me, Jen. We need to get some fluids into her and some steroids. I think she injured herself with all that pushing while the foal was stuck."

Jenny sprinted to the office to alert the vet techs. Within minutes Meghan and Paul, two of the night-time technicians, had Sunny on IV fluids and dexamethasone.[1]

Dr. Andrews started milking Sunny.

"What are you doing?" Jenny demanded.

"We need to get as much colostrum[2] from her as we can, Jen. Your foal will need it or we may lose her too."

Jenny crumpled, weeping. She crawled over to Sunny's face. "Sunny, don't die. You can't. This sweet baby needs you, and so do I."

Sunny didn't move or blink. Her eyes were fixed, staring straight ahead. *Is she breathing?* The thought almost choked Jenny. *Yes, there it is. The rise and fall.*

Jenny stroked the mare's face, sobbing.

"Miss Thomas," Meghan said, "we *must* get you out of here. Dr. Andrews needs to help Sunny. Let's get your filly and you to another stall where you'll be safe. Marcus will move the foal."

Marcus swooped up the filly in his huge arms, and Meghan grabbed the foaling kit. Jenny walked in a daze, empty-handed, to a stall across the hall. *I can't believe this is happening, Lord. Why is this happening?*

Do you trust Me?

Yes, Lord.

Do you trust Me enough to want what I want even when it doesn't look like what you want?

Yes, her heart answered after it quieted. *Sunny is yours, Lord. Thank you that I can trust you no matter what happens.*

Enjoy this filly. I have made perfect provision for Sunny.

Jenny pulled the baby into her lap. *She is so small and perfect—well, small compared to Sunny. Please, Sunny, live. I want you to meet this baby.*

"Jen," Dr. Andrews called. "Go ahead and finish imprinting[3] your filly. I *promise* I'll let you know if something happens here."

Jenny fought to remember the order in which she had wanted to do the parts of the imprinting. Her eyes filled with tears as she tried to coordinate her left and right hands. *First I want to touch the filly all over with my hands.*

Jenny thought about her mentor and instructor in Pennsylvania, Colton Wright. He was the wise horse trainer who had totally changed her understanding about horses. Colton's words of advice echoed in her mind. *"You've got about two hours, Jen, to imprint upon that foal. Those critical hours are created by God to teach that foal who is safe and who is*

enemy. The foal will imprint on the mama horse, and then later, the herd. You don't want to interfere with the mare and foal. You just want to be there as well, to become part of that foal's "herd." So start out with approach and retreat, just like we did with Fury. Watch the way Sunny treats the foal. She'll lick him or her and love on that foal. You do the same with your hands. Just handle that baby with love. Then when you can rub that baby all over, start adding other stimuli like plastic bags, clippers, and so on. You want to remove the bag when the foal relaxes. Not before. You can do more harm than good if you reward fear."

"Sure wish you were here, Colton," Jenny said aloud. "I could use some help right about now."

I am here.

Lord? Jenny's heart questioned. *How is it that You can be here with me and with everyone else in the world who needs You? Even folks who don't love You. You must be there with them too.*

Look outside at the stars in the sky. How many do you see?

Jenny peeked out through the small window of the equine hospital. Even through the tiny square she saw more stars than she could count.

I placed each star perfectly. A higher number than a human being can comprehend. The population of the earth is a number that can be counted by people. It is so small to Me it is like the number one to you.

"Oh," she gasped, overwhelmed as she understood.

Who do you think created imprinting?

You, Lord, of course, Jenny prayed with a grin.

Enjoy your filly. I am here and will never leave you.

Jenny placed her fingers in the foal's toothless mouth. The little tongue flicked up reflexively. Jenny felt a tug as the filly's tongue curled around her index finger and started suckling. Jenny touched the filly's gums, tongue, and lips. She rubbed each part gently until she felt the baby's body relax. Then she moved quietly on to the next area.

The filly took a two-minute nap, her eyelids closing slowly. Her muzzle drooped little by little until it contacted the shavings. Her little neck jerked as she was startled awake. She looked around like someone who fell asleep during a sermon and snored themselves awake.

Adorable. Impossible to resist.

The filly tried to get her unbelievably long legs to work. They were uncooperative, flying in all directions at once. She got the front ones out and up. She sat back like a dog for a moment before totally collapsing. Her front legs landed on the right side of her, her back legs to the left. She stayed there a moment then heaved up again. She made it halfway up before crashing onto her side.

Jenny glanced at the clock on the wall. *Half an hour? Is that all?* It was almost four-fifteen. Almost time for the birds to start greeting the day.

The filly pushed her nose into Jenny's hand insistently. Jenny rubbed the damp mane and neck then stood back as the foal launched another attempt to stand. She got the front legs out again, sat for a moment, and then popped her fanny up. She was standing! After about three seconds, she fell again. The third attempt was more coordinated, and the foal stood for a while, swaying. Then without warning her legs buckled, and she collapsed.

Jenny sat behind the filly, rubbing her neck, inviting her to lie flat on her side. The foal tried to roll up once, then sighed and settled back down.

Tears sprang to Jenny's eyes and fell unnoticed. She leaned forward, gently stroking the filly's face. *Her eyelashes are ridiculous. Long and feathery.* The eyelashes fluttered open for a moment, and wise infant eyes gazed into Jenny's.

Marcus cleared his throat loudly. "Yep, you're gone, smitten, in love, totally gone," he teased.

Jenny could only shake her head with wonder.

"Let's get Sunny's colostrum into her," Marcus suggested. "I'll get the bottle."

"Sweet baby, I haven't even named you," Jenny whispered. "None of the names I chose will fit."

She tried some out loud. "Sonrise Gold? No. Jenny's Sonrise . . . no. I give up. One will come to me, I'm sure."

Marcus returned with the bottle. "Did you say something?" he quipped.

"No, just thinking out loud," she replied.

"I'll check on Sunny," he said. "Be right back."

Jenny smiled her thanks as she took the bottle. She watched entranced as the filly's pink tongue curled around the artificial teat of the bottle. The filly drank the bottle dry. The liquid seemed to strengthen her, and she attempted to rise once again.

Marcus returned with news. "They're still working on Sunny," he said, shrugging. "Dr. Andrews is still not sure what happened. It looks like she has some nerve damage from straining."

The filly got her front legs up and out, swaying back and forth. She then overbalanced and crashed sideways into the shavings.

Jenny's arms reached out spontaneously every time the filly fell. It was all she could do to keep from grabbing the foal.

"Don't help her. She needs to stand on her own," Marcus warned.

"I know," Jenny replied, unable to tear her eyes away from the foal. "It's an automatic reaction."

She's almost there.

"Well," Marcus began, smiling as he watched. "We'll need to treat her like an orphan. I'll get a nursemare for her."

"What's a nursemare?"

"A nursemare is a mare who has foaled recently. We take her baby away and bring the mare in to be a mama for your foal."

"What happens to the nursemare's baby?" Jenny inquired.

"Dunno," Marcus said a little too casually.

"Yes, you do," she said, narrowing her eyes. "Tell me."

"Raising an orphan is very difficult," he began. "You don't even want to go there."

"Tell me," she insisted.

"All right," he huffed. "They are usually sold at auction. Most of the meat is exported overseas, where it's considered a delicacy."

"What?" she shrieked, startling the filly. "No way. Not ever."

"You will lose *this* baby if we don't do it," Marcus said dryly. "Doesn't it make sense to sacrifice a foal worth nothing to save a foal this valuable?"

"No," she thundered. "No, it does not make sense. God is the one in charge of life and death. If this baby survives, it will be because of Him. You tell me what I need to do, and I'll do it."

"Jenny," Marcus said, trying to sound firm, "that's what these nursemares are for. That is their purpose."

"Marcus," Jenny replied just as firmly, "I don't care. I will not take one life for another. Won't do it."

"All right," he conceded, shrugging. "You win. I'll mix up some formula for your foal. She's going to need it."

"Thank you," she answered coldly.

"It's going to be fine, little one," Jenny crooned to the baby. "I've done this once before, with your mama. We'll make it."

The filly had worn herself out. After a bottle of warm formula, she fell sound asleep across Jenny's outstretched legs.

Jenny leaned against the stall wall. Her eyelids were heavy weights. She tried to keep them open, but her eyes just crossed. *Must stay awake for Sunny*, she chastised herself.

Do you trust Me?

Yes, Lord, why do you ask? She felt stung by the question.

Do you trust me like that?

Jenny gazed again at the filly. Completely trusting, oblivious to the crisis around her, she lay asleep in the lap of a "predator."

Yes, Lord.

Then sleep. I have it under control.

Jenny shifted gently onto her side and curled up around the foal in the deep shavings. The filly stirred slightly, pressing into her.

Hot morning light beamed like a laser directly onto Jenny's closed right eyelid. The inside of her eye began to burn. Instinctively her hand came up to shade it. She felt disoriented and exhausted. Her mouth felt like sawdust. "A couple more minutes," she mumbled to no one. She moved her head slightly and brought her hand back down onto soft baby hair. *Hair! The filly. Sunny.*

It all rushed back to her mind. She gazed at the sleeping filly in her arms. Jenny lay still, feeling drowsy. She blinked sleepily and craned her neck around to see what time it was. *Seven o'clock. Two hours of sleep.* Her left arm was under the foal and had gone completely numb. Jenny lay still, just watching the rise and fall of the filly's breathing.

Look outside.

Jenny looked up and out the window. A gasp escaped her throat as she took in the glorious sunrise. Pink, orange, yellow, and lavender swirled together like a watercolor painting. Wispy pink-white clouds looked like horse tails high in the sky.

Awed, she struggled to sit up, disturbing the filly in the process. The baby launched her own struggle to rise. She gathered her legs under her and then heaved up, standing shakily. She overbalanced, but instead of crashing, she took her first tottering steps.

Sunlight streamed through her curly little mane like a halo. The filly stood in the light, eyes closed, basking in the warm rays.

Glory.

"Glory!" Jenny whispered. The name was so obvious. "Morning Glory Sonrise. We'll call you Glory."

Glory responded with a tiny whinny, the first sound Jenny had heard her make. The filly took a few more shaky steps before crashing headfirst into the deep shavings.

Sunny whickered from the stall across the way. Jenny leapt up and threw the door back.

"Sunny!" Jenny shrieked joyfully.

---

[1] A steroid commonly used in horses.

[2] Colostrum is a rich, yellow fluid food that the baby drinks from the mother's mammary glands during the first few days after birth.

[3] A method of training in the first 48 hours of a foal's life. It teaches the foal to accept human beings with little or no fear. In general, horses think of human beings as predators.

Chapter Three

Jenny didn't even think to close Glory's stall door. She raced across the hall to Sunny's door, throwing it open. Sunny rolled herself onto her sternum. The big mare whickered again, and Glory bumped against Jenny's legs. Before Jenny could blink, the baby tottered over to Sunny's head and began nuzzling and whickering. Sunny threw herself to the left, trying to rise.

"Get the filly outta there," Dr. Andrews ordered, rushing around the corner. "Sunny *needs* to be down. We certainly don't want anyone getting crushed if she gets up and falls."

Dr. Andrews swooped up Glory into his arms and marched across the hall to her stall.

"Here's the deal, Jenny," he explained, smiling as he watched the filly wobble around on her unsteady legs. He brought his eyes back to Jenny's, and his expression turned serious. "Sunny sustained some nerve damage when the filly was stuck. She pushed so hard, we're fortunate the baby wasn't damaged. Anyway, what Sunny needs now is several days of complete rest so that we can see how much function she'll get back."

"What do you mean by 'function'?" Jenny asked. "Will she be able to jump again?"

"Only time will tell," Dr. Andrews replied. "If I had to guess, I would say no. Certainly not at the level she did before."

"Well, I don't care," Jenny replied. "I'm just glad she's still here with me . . . with us. Me and Glory."

"And who is Glory?" inquired Dr. Andrews.

Jenny grinned. "Morning Glory Sonrise. The newest addition to Sonrise Farm Too!"

"Sonrise Farm Two?" Dr. Andrews questioned, holding up two fingers in a peace sign.

"No, Sonrise Farm Too, as in 'also.' It was Kathy's idea. Kathy is my instructor and close friend at home. Sort of a play on words."

"OK, I get it," the vet said, smiling. "Here's what we need to do. Let's get these girls next door to each other, so Sunny can see her baby. She looks really interested in her, but we can't have them together yet. Not until Sunny can stand without falling. You milk Sunny every two hours to keep her supply going. Then as soon as she can safely stand, we'll see if she will accept Glory. That would be the best-case scenario for everyone, especially you," Dr. Andrews said with a grin. "You think you're tired now? Just wait till you're four weeks into raising an orphan."

They got to work pulling down the dividing wall between Sunny's stall and the one next door. Then they picked up a metal screen partition and installed it between the stalls.

"I think that will work!" Dr. Andrews chortled. "Now it's up to the girls. Let's get Glory in here and see what happens."

Sunny and Glory spent a full hour whickering back and forth. Jenny and three strong vet techs managed to pull Sunny closer to the barrier. Sunny stretched her long neck, trying to lick Glory's face. The filly mashed her nose against the small holes in the screen partition. Sunny licked the little nose through the screen until she grew exhausted. Then with a sigh she lay flat on her side and slept.

Over the next three days Jenny and the vet techs rolled Sunny over every two hours so she wouldn't get sores. After they rolled her, Jenny would milk her. Then they propped her up with bales of straw.

"How much longer, Dr. Andrews?" Jenny asked after lunch as she transferred Sunny's milk to a sterile container for Glory.

"Another day and we'll see where we are. I'm hoping Sunny will be standing soon . . . really soon."

Glory's high-pitched whinny echoed in the hallway. Jenny bolted toward the filly's stall and saw Sunny, back on her haunches, trying to rise.

"Dr. Andrews!" she shrieked joyfully. "She's trying to get up!"

He jogged over, smiling. "This is why I get the big bucks." He slid the stall door open, grabbing a lead rope on the way in. He approached Sunny cautiously. The big mare groaned and sank back onto the floor. "Hey, Sunny," Dr. Andrews said softly, rubbing her powerful neck. "Let me help you." He reached down and clipped the lead rope to her halter. Sunny gathered herself once more. Dr. Andrews pulled sideways and back toward Sunny's tail.

What is he doing? Jenny wondered.

The vet's steady pull gave the mare just enough counterbalance. She took a huge breath, got her front legs out in front of her, and heaved herself up. The mare overbalanced and leaned dangerously to the right. Just when it looked as though she would fall, she took three wild, scrambling steps to the right, careening into the white cinderblock wall. It held her up.

Sunny stayed plastered against the wall for several seconds. Her wild eyes were fixed straight ahead as though *any* movement would make her lose her balance.

Jenny's fingernails had splinters of wood under them from digging into Sunny's door as she watched. She glanced down at them, realizing one was actually bleeding. She shook her hands and sucked in a deep breath. *The splinter will have to wait.*

Moment by moment Sunny relaxed. Finally she blew out a big breath through her nostrils. It sounded like "whew." Jenny smiled a tiny smile.

"That's it, girl. Lean on the wall."

Sunny turned her head at the sound of Jenny's voice.

"This is the most dangerous point," Dr. Andrews warned. "She can and *will* fall at any time. You and Glory *must* stay out of this stall until she is stronger. Do you understand?"

Jenny nodded silently, staring at Sunny.

"You are my sunshine, my only sunshine," she sang quietly. "You make me happy when skies are gray. You'll never know, dear, how much I love you. Please don't take my Sunny away."

The mare swiveled her ears back, listening to Jenny. Slowly, inch by inch, the mare shifted her weight from the wall. Little by little she gained confidence.

"I will be here, Sunny. I will not leave you," Jenny promised.

The mare stayed near the wall, legs shaking as she transferred all her weight over her feet. At last she stood alone, shakier than her filly but standing.

"Get the mare a couple buckets of water," Dr. Andrews directed Meghan. "Be very cautious. We don't want her overbalancing on you."

Meghan filled a red bucket from the spigot outside Sunny's stall. Sunny licked her lips as she heard the bucket handle clank. Her knees shook, nearly buckling as Meghan slid the stall door open. Sunny carefully lowered her head as the bucket arrived. She drank and drank. After emptying two buckets, the mare sighed and leaned against the wall once more.

Several hours later, Dr. Andrews came back to check on Sunny.

"She hasn't moved," Jenny stated as the vet approached.

"She can't stay there forever, Jen. She *will* fall. I just hope she doesn't hurt herself in the process."

But she didn't fall.

Jenny and Glory kept watch from the neighboring stall all day. Sunny moved very little. She seemed to be experimenting with shifting weight from the wall to her own feet.

Meghan checked on her at dinner time. "How is she, Jen?"

"Hasn't really moved," Jenny replied. "She shifts her weight but hasn't moved her feet."

"She knows what she's doing," Meghan said. "I'll get her more water."

Jenny gazed at Glory, who could now move her feet in almost any direction she chose. The same feet that had appeared to have minds of their own were now coordinating and working together. She trotted and cantered around the spacious stall.

A low whicker from Sunny brought Jenny's eyes back to the other stall. The mare pushed away from the wall and stood swaying slightly. She picked up her right front foot and quickly plopped it back down. She tried again. This time she managed to gain several inches. She carefully moved her weight forward. Her left foot came off the ground, and she took her first step.

Glory turned toward her mother and let out a high-pitched baby whinny. Sunny kept coming, inching her way to the barrier between her and the filly. Her eyes were on Glory.

Jenny could only hold her breath. Her hand automatically covered her mouth. She watched, unblinking, as the two made their way. *Please don't fall, Sunny,* she thought.

They met at the dividing wall and stood nose to nose. Sunny whickered, a low, rich sound. The filly danced in place, nuzzling and pushing on the screen.

Restoration.

What? Jenny's heart asked.

I will restore all that seemed lost.

What do you mean, Lord?

You will see.

Chapter Four

Jenny moved her cot into Glory's stall so that she could see Sunny through the screen partition. As she drifted off to sleep, she saw Sunny's shadow standing at the wall, nose to the divider. Glory slept soundly near Sunny. Jenny woke several times, flicking on a pocket flashlight each time. Sunny stood like a statue in the same spot.

Memories stirred in Jenny's mind.

They were at the big arena in Washington, D.C. Sunny snorted impatiently, dancing in place. Jenny asked the big mare to bend her powerful neck to the left. As Sunny sniffed the toe of Jenny's left boot, Jenny slipped the bridle off the mare's head and dropped it. Then Jenny focused hard on the jump ahead—the world's tallest wall. "We're gonna do it, Sunny," she breathed. And the mare exploded from the ground in a dizzying 7-foot, 9-inch leap. The applause was
. . . quietly rustling?

Jenny's eyes popped open. Morning poured in through the bare hospital windows. Sunny had moved. The rustlings were from Sunny's hind toes dragging the ground as she paced up and down the partition dividing the stalls.

Jenny unzipped the sleeping bag and started to scramble out. She caught her big toe in the bag and tumbled off the cot. Jumping up without brushing shavings from her sweat pants, she took two running steps and hit the emergency buzzer on the wall. She stood quietly waiting for Dr. Andrews. *She's dragging those toes, but she looks steady!*

"What do you think?" Jenny blurted out as the vet rounded the corner.

"Hold your horses!" he grinned, spying her shavings-covered sweats. "Let me do a quick assessment." Dr. Andrews slid the stall door open. Sunny stopped pacing and turned her neck to see him. "Hey, girl," he greeted softly. Sunny turned her eyes back to her sleeping filly.

"Jen, call her. I want to see how she moves."

Jenny walked to the other end of Glory's stall and whistled softly. Glory startled at the sound and lifted her head from the soft shavings. Sunny moved toward Jenny.

"Now, go to the other end and call her. I want to see if she can negotiate the turn," the vet directed.

Jenny jogged to the other end of the partition and whistled softly again. Glory jumped up to join the game.

"This is a regular dog-and-pony show," Dr. Andrews said, laughing as the filly bucked playfully behind Jenny.

Sunny stopped for a moment before actually turning. It seemed that she was deciding the best direction to go. Slowly and deliberately she turned to the left. As her body curved into the turn her right hock twisted out from under her. She shuffled her front legs to counterbalance and stood swaying for several seconds.

Dr. Andrews and Jenny stood planted, waiting, not breathing. Would she fall? Finally the mare lifted a front hoof to continue the turn. Jenny could see the mighty chest muscles straining as Sunny figured out how to compensate for her weak hindquarters. The left hind seemed weaker than the right. It almost caught several times as Sunny marched slowly back toward Jenny. *Not pretty, but done*, Jenny breathed, placing her hand on her pounding heart as Sunny reached her.

Dr. Andrews and Sunny let out a sigh at the same time.

"Can you take that one more time, Jen?" asked the vet.

"I guess so," Jenny responded.

"Whenever you are ready."

The second trip up and back was easier for everyone. By the third trip Sunny had clearly determined the easiest way to turn with her hind legs.

"All right, I think she's stable enough to be with her filly," Dr. Andrews announced, looking pleased. "She obviously wants to, and Glory is certainly strong and quick enough to move if she needs to get out of the way. Let's try it."

Jenny placed the foal halter on Glory's head and attached the lead rope. The filly did not want to leave the stall, and she sat on her haunches. Jenny closed her fingers slowly, adding more and more steady pressure forward. All of a sudden the filly straightened her hind legs. Jenny's hands sprang open to release the forward pressure on the halter. The filly licked her lips, staring at Jenny with ears pricked forward.

"Let's try again, little one," Jenny urged, taking up the slack in the lead rope. This time the filly sat back just slightly. Again Jenny closed her fingers slowly, increasing the pressure gradually until she felt the filly shift forward. *Release. It's the release that teaches.* Colton's words rang in Jenny's ears.

The third time Jenny coaxed the filly forward, Glory went easily. She followed Jenny toward the stall door, whinnying her high-pitched baby call as they went through. Glory heard her own hooves strike the concrete, and she scared herself. She sat back against the halter again.

"Come on, baby," Jenny said with a smile, repeating the process. "We're going to see Sunny."

Sunny trumpeted, and Glory surged forward. The filly trotted several steps, tail up, hooves clacking as she hurried toward the sound. Jenny stopped at Sunny's door and slid it open. The mare turned carefully, eyes bright, ears forward. Jenny slipped the halter off Glory's face and watched the reunion with tears of joy.

Even Dr. Andrews had to wipe his eyes a couple of times. "Boy, Jen. It's a relief to see that! I wasn't certain we'd have a happy ending to this one."

Sunny whickered low, nuzzling Glory's face. The filly nudged back, seeking with her nose. She found Sunny's swollen udder and had her first meal without a bottle.

Jenny allowed herself to sink down into the shavings and watch. *Thank you Lord,* her soul sang.

After a hot bath, a warm lunch, and a phone call home, Jenny shook her sleeping bag out in the now empty stall next to Sunny's. *A little nap on the shavings will do me good,* she thought. *I sure won't miss that yucky cot.*

She curled up in the corner closest to Sunny's stall. She could see both mother and baby but wouldn't get trampled by sharp little hooves as Glory romped.

She was just starting to give in to the floating comfort of sleep when a sharp voice pierced the peacefulness of the foaling wing.

"I *know* I don't have much time," she heard Marcus say in a low angry tone. "What do you want from me? I disconnected the buzzer and the video camera. I've done everything you told me to do. It's not so easy. That girl never leaves. She sleeps on a cot in the hall."

Jenny sat up quietly, pulling her legs in tight. She scrunched against the wall and held her breath as she heard Marcus approach Sunny's stall. She could almost feel his eyes searching.

Please keep him from seeing me, Lord.

"Yeah, I'm sure she's not here," Marcus growled. "She's got to eat sometime."

He's going to hear my pounding heart! she thought.

"Tomorrow it is," Marcus said.

Jenny heard the door to the foaling wing swing shut before she allowed herself to exhale. Jenny's mind raced. *I've got to call home . . . now! I've got to get Sunny and Glory out of here!*

A few moments later she was trying to explain what she had heard to Dr. Andrews.

"But I heard him!" Jenny insisted. "He was talking to someone, I have *no* doubt who, about hurting Sunny."

Dr. Andrews rubbed his forehead gingerly as though it was pounding inside. "I find it almost impossible to . . . Why? Why would Vanessa DuBois risk getting caught? She is one of the largest financial contributors to this hospital. Do you know what this would do to her reputation?"

"Think about it," Jenny implored. "Who else could it be?"

"But," Dr. Andrews argued, "who disabled the camera and buzzer?"

Jenny shrugged. "Marcus. I heard him say so."

Dr. Andrews gave a tired sigh. "Marcus has been with us only a couple of weeks. He arrived three days before you and Sunny."

Jenny waited for his answer.

"All right," Dr. Andrews said decisively. "You stay here with your horses. I agree that you should take them home *now*. I can work with Dr. Davis to oversee Sunny's recovery at Sonrise Farm. Don't call home yet though. I need to make certain everything is secure. Our phone lines may be bugged."

Jenny stood next to Sunny as Dr. Andrews slipped out.

"Paul! Meghan!" he bellowed as he strode down the hall, "you two go help Jenny Thomas with her mare."

In seconds the two vet techs were at Jenny's side. "What do you need, Miss Thomas?" Paul asked.

"Would you help get us packed?" Jenny requested casually, though her heart was thumping. "We're going home. All of us." *Boy that sounds nice,* she thought, smiling.

Dr. Andrews returned with his cell phone. "Now call," he said, hitting the On button as he handed it through the bars of the stall. "We'll *all* wait here with you until your ride arrives."

"But it will take them two hours to get here!" Jenny exclaimed. "Don't you have things to do?"

"Jenny," Dr. Andrews spoke seriously again. "We need to keep your horses safe. There are other vets here. They know I'm tied up for a while. I'd call the police but I—I'm not sure what to do. If I call the police and file a complaint against our largest contributor and I'm wrong . . . well, I think you can see how disastrous that would be. We need to conduct an investigation ourselves first and see if we have enough evidence. Otherwise I think she'll just slip through the judicial cracks again."

Jenny nodded agreement as she punched the number for Sonrise Farm.

"Hello, Sonrise Farm, Kathy speaking."

"Kathy! They're letting Sunny go home today with the baby. Can you bring the slantload¹?"

"Really? That's great," Kathy said, chortling. "I'll send Daniel. My next lesson just arrived."

"Oh," Jenny answered, trying not to sound disappointed. Her heart dropped as she imagined what she would say to Daniel, the same Daniel who not so long ago had *helped* Vanessa DuBois. *He's Vanessa's nephew. I know he's changed, spent the year with Colton and all, but . . .*

"Is that all right?" Kathy asked, picking up on Jenny's tone. "Daniel just pulled in from Colton's, so his rig is all hooked up."

"Yeah, it's fine," Jenny said, trying to sound happy. "But please have him hook up the slantload. Sunny's going to need the extra support." She paused a moment. "I just really wanted to talk with *you* on the way home."

"Can we talk when you get back?"

"Sure," Jenny sighed.

---

[1]A slantload trailer allows horses to travel facing the side of the trailer. It also allows a large open space for foals to travel.

Chapter Five

"Jenny! Sunny! Oh, sorry, didn't mean to disturb the baby." Daniel breezed in and gave Jenny a brotherly hug. She noticed that he smelled like after-shave and horse sweat, and his cheek was bristly against hers.

"Oh, man. She's gorgeous, Jen. Look at those legs! They're a mile long! And she's a palomino like her mama."

Jenny watched Daniel as he watched the filly. He looked tanned and rested after his long apprenticeship with Colton Wright. It was difficult to remember him as Vanessa DuBois' groom and helper and nephew. *He has completely transformed,* she realized.

"How are things at Colton's place?" Jenny inquired.

"Fabuloso," Daniel said, beaming. "It's been an incredible time. And you will not believe how great Fury looks!"

"Can't wait to see him," Jenny said briskly. "Let's load up and get going. The sooner the better."

"Yeah," drawled Daniel. "They're calling for thunderstorms later. I'd sure like to miss those. I hate hauling horses in the rain."

Daniel led Glory into the trailer and connected the first divider. The foal whinnied frantically. Sunny lunged into the trailer, dragging Jenny with her. "Whoa, girl, we're not stealing your baby," Jenny assured the mare. "See? There she is, right next to you."

Sunny put her long neck over the divider to nuzzle Glory, and the filly settled down immediately. The mare snatched a mouthful of hay from the hay bag[1] and munched contentedly.

Jenny stroked Sunny's face, satisfied that the horses were secure. "Have a good ride, girls. See you in a couple hours."

Daniel drove the big rig slowly around the circular driveway. Jenny waved to Dr. Andrews and the rest of the staff. Marcus rushed out as they pulled away, and Jenny saw a panicked look on his face.

"I wonder what he'll do now," she thought aloud.

"Who?" asked Daniel. "What are you rambling about? You *must* be sleep-deprived, bottle feeding that monstrous filly."

"Actually, she's nursing. Sunny accepted her even though they'd been apart for three days."

"Wow!" Daniel breathed, impressed. "What a sweet mare. So other than the near-death experience, how was your first foaling?" he inquired playfully.

"A little weird, Daniel," Jenny said softly.

"How so?"

"Well, this vet tech named Marcus disconnected the emergency call buzzer *and* the foaling camera in Sunny's stall."

"Why would he do that?" Daniel asked, and then realized the answer on his own. "No! Not Aunt Vanessa!" he exclaimed. "Do you really think—?"

"Who else?" Jenny said, shrugging.

"Then she's lost her mind," he stated firmly. "We have

to go to the police, Jenny. She'll stop at nothing."

"Agreed. As soon as we get home I'll have my Dad call."

Jenny gazed out the window of the noisy dually.[2] The tires beat out a mind-numbing rhythm, and her eyelids began to droop. She allowed the stress and turmoil of the day to fall away. *We're safe now,* she kept saying to herself. She closed her eyes and dozed.

A loud explosion startled her awake. "What was that?" she gasped, blinking groggily.

"Thunder," Daniel replied.

A huge lightning bolt struck so close that it rattled the windows. Big, hard raindrops pounded the windshield. Jenny glanced at her watch. It was 4:15.

"Kind of like a power wash for the truck," Daniel quipped, trying to sound lighthearted. His knuckles were white on the steering wheel. "I hate hauling in the rain," he muttered under his breath.

Jenny glanced behind her at the trailer. "Windows in the trailer closed?" she asked.

Daniel nodded. "They're cozy, and we're fine. I don't like it. It doesn't mean I can't do it."

Jenny watched an oncoming car as it approached. It was speeding and having trouble staying on the rain-slick road. *What is that driver thinking?* her brain shrieked as the blue sedan began straddling the center dividing line of the road.

Daniel braked as the car continued into their lane.

"Get out of my way, you idiot!" he shouted at the driver, flashing his lights and honking. Finally he desperately pulled the rig to the right. He struggled to maintain control as the wheels slid onto the gravel shoulder. The other vehicle continued straight toward them.

"*No!*" he shouted.

The oncoming car pulled back into its lane at the last moment. It was a familiar blue Mercedes that flew past them.

Jenny felt the hair on the back of her neck stand straight up. "Daniel," she whispered. "That was Vanessa." She stared into the passenger-side mirror. She saw the Mercedes spin around in a barely controlled 180-degree turn. It stayed on their tail for a moment, then shot past, horn blaring. Jenny craned her neck and caught Vanessa's maniacal expression.

"Daniel, give me the cell phone. I'm calling the police *now*!"

She stared at the phone and punched 911. Nothing. No dial tone, no ring, nothing.

"It's not working," she croaked. "What do we do?"

Jenny looked around desperately. They were on a back road with no house in sight, just pine trees and weeds as far as the eye could see. Ominous dark clouds filling the sky made it look like approaching night. A strange greenish tinge caused Jenny to shiver. Then the rain stopped for a moment.

"We may have bigger trouble than Aunt Vanessa," Daniel said, peering through the windshield. "This almost looks like tornado weather. Jen, keep your eyes peeled for a bridge to stop under."

Jenny glanced at the cell phone again. *Still no reception. Great!*

Then a wall of rain hit them like a wave. It buffeted the truck, making conversation impossible.

Daniel slowed down to forty miles per hour. The rain was coming down so fast that the ditches beside the road quickly overflowed. The road itself became a clay-colored river. The truck hit a huge puddle, causing it to lurch and splashing red silty water against Jenny's window.

"Slow down, Daniel!" Jenny shrieked over the din of the pounding rain. "You'll get the horses wet. The trailer just has floorboards, you know."

"I know, Jen," Daniel yelled back. "But I'm afraid we're in for more than just rain. We need to find a bridge. Fast!"

"Oh," Jenny gasped, getting his drift. She clicked on the radio full blast and heard an announcer speaking.

"Again, for those who missed the earlier report, there has been a tornado sighted in the region. Please head for your basement or other underground shelter. If you are driving, find a bridge or leave your vehicle and take cover in a ditch."

The rain was coming down so hard now, it seemed determined to shatter the windshield. Daniel had the wipers on warp speed, but they could not keep up with the deluge. Then the rain became hail the size of walnuts. The din of the hailstones drowned out the radio, even though Jenny had turned it to full volume. Trees were bending like twigs, lightning flashed, and thunder crashed close enough for Jenny and Daniel to feel the vibrations of it. To the right of the road, thick power lines had broken and were whipping about like venomous snakes.

Lord, keep us safe, Jenny implored. *Keep the horses safe.*

"Jen," Daniel yelled. "I think I see a bridge up there. Can you see it?"

She pulled herself forward, almost to the dashboard, straining to focus her eyes through the sea of hail and rain. "I see *something* ahead," she concurred. "What is it?"

She sucked in a scream. A twister, huge and dragonlike, touched down with a roar two hundred yards away. A wave of branches and debris pelted the truck. A huge stone smashed against the windshield, leaving a circular shatter mark right in the middle. The twister raged across the road before disappearing up into the trees.

Daniel slowed the truck and followed the twister with his eyes for a moment. Jenny looked down to see a mammoth pine tree across the road directly in front of them. Daniel slammed the brakes to the floor. The truck hydroplaned sideways as Daniel clung to the wheel helplessly. Something threw Jenny back into the seat, and her seat belt tightened. Her arms flew up reflexively to protect her face as they approached the enormous tree.

"Sunny!" she screamed. Then blackness.

---

[1] A large pickup truck with dual wheels at the back.

[2] A hay bag is a rope bag large enough to hold several flakes of hay. Hay bags are hung at face level in stalls or trailers.

Chapter Six

"Jenny, are you all right?" Someone was rubbing her left arm, and it hurt. The radio was blaring loudly, and the windshield wipers were squealing at full speed. *Where am I? Why am I wet?* she thought.

She tried to brush the hand away, but the voice was insistent. "Jen, wake up. We crashed. I need help with Sunny."

"Sunny!" Jenny's eyes flew open. She saw pine needles and water in the cab. The front of the truck was invisible, buried in the middle of the gigantic pine tree. A limb had torn the roof open, allowing rain to soak them and the seats. She and Daniel were both still buckled in.

Jenny saw that Daniel had a bloody gash on his forehead and a quickly swelling upper lip. "I think my front tooth is loose," he said, feeling it with his tongue. "We need to get out of here and check on the horses."

Jenny shook her head a little. Her left arm felt sore, as though it had a muscle strain. Her right arm seemed OK, so she reached across and unbuckled her seatbelt. It was so tight that it felt like removing a horse's girth. She ducked her head under the pine branch and slid out the door. Her legs held her up. She tottered around to the rear of the trailer.

It's still up! she thought. At least it hadn't turned over. "Sunny?" she whispered loudly. *I almost don't want to see,* she realized. *How can they not be dead?*

Sunny nickered. *Yes!*

I am the Lord of Life and death, He reminded her.

Yes, Lord, you are. And she flung the door wide.

Sunny turned and gazed at Jenny. The mare had a scrape on her nose, and the halter had snapped in two places, cutting her cheek. "Thank you, God, that we used the slantload," Jenny whispered, imagining the scene had the horses been loose in the stock trailer.

A close inspection of Glory revealed a scratch on her nose and nothing more.

Jenny sank to the floor of the trailer and watched the two for a moment. She pulled herself upright and rubbed Sunny's neck, studying her. *Thank you, Lord. I think they are really OK.*

"Well, they look really good, Daniel," she announced. She waited for his reply.

"Daniel?" Jenny hopped out of the trailer and closed the door. She rushed to the driver's side of the truck. The door was open, the seat empty. "Daniel, where are you?" she screamed.

"Jenny! Over here! I need help!" His frantic voice sent a chill up her spine.

"Where are you?"

"On the other side of the tree!"

"How do I get there?" Jenny screamed back. *There is no going through this tree!*

"Go around, and hurry!" he shouted.

The tree had been completely uprooted, and the root ball was at least 10 feet high. Jenny glanced at it as she ran past. A gaping red crater in the clay revealed where the mighty evergreen had stood for decades. The scent of pine and dirt blew about Jenny's nostrils. The wind gusted violently, making the tree creak painfully. *It sounds like it's suffering*, she thought. And then she saw Daniel leaning into a navy blue Mercedes. He straightened up, his face ashen. "It's Aunt Vanessa. I think she's dead."

Jenny pushed him aside. The woman inside *looked* dead. Jenny felt for a pulse. Nothing. She glanced at Daniel. He had turned away. *CPR. I took that Red Cross CPR class at church when I worked in the nursery. That was a couple years ago. Can I remember how?* For a moment, a battle raged inside Jenny. *What do I care if she's dead? After all she's done to me and Sunny.*

I care. I love her.

Quickly Jenny tilted the driver's seat back all the way and began CPR on her enemy, Vanessa DuBois.

One, two, three chest compressions, pinch the nostrils, puff into the mouth. One, two, three compressions, puff. One, two, three . . .

Jenny continued until she felt dizzy. *Can't stop. Must continue.* She tried to focus but was unable.

"Jenny, that's enough. Stop." Daniel insisted. "You're going to fall over." He took her arm, pulling gently. "You really tried. Let her go."

She was just about to give up when she felt the gasp. She checked for a pulse. *Faint but there.* Jenny stared intently at Vanessa's face. The ice-blue eyes snapped open and stared at her. "Get off me! What are you doing here?" Vanessa hissed weakly.

Jenny moved backwards and straightened up, rubbing her aching back. "You were in a crash. I was trying to help you."

Daniel broke in, "She just saved your life, Aunt V."

"Well then. Help me get out of here," she ordered.

Daniel poked his head back into the driver's side. He

shook his head and pulled Jenny aside. "Her legs are crushed under the dashboard. There's no way we're getting her out. We need real help."

"What'll we do?" Jenny asked.

"I don't know. The cell phone is dead. The truck is not driveable, and the nearest town is at least fifteen miles away. I wish I'd taken I-95 instead of this back route. What about the horses? Could I ride Sunny?"

"Sure, and take Glory with you?"

"Oh, yeah," he replied. "Well, somehow I've got to get help. And fast."

"What should *I* do?" she asked.

"You stay here with her, since you're the one who knows CPR. Stay with her, and I'll start hiking to the nearest phone. And pray, Jen."

"Hurry," Jenny urged.

Now what, Lord? she asked. *Who do I spend my energy on? The horses need me and so does . . . she.*

The horses are fine.

Jenny battled the wind-swept pine branches and needles to get to the passenger side of the blue Mercedes. She had her hand on the door handle and was about to open it when a tiny peeping sound drew her eyes to the left. She saw, still nestled in the limbs, a sparrow's nest. It was tilting like the *Titanic*, ready to go head first into the sea. Mama sparrow sat in the middle, glaring ferociously at Jenny. The little bird puffed her feathers to make herself look as terrifying as possible.

"I need to move your family, Mama Bird. Someone will be along to cut down this tree someday." *Are we all alone on this road?* she wondered, looking around. *Why doesn't someone drive by or at least drive up to the tree?* The clouds above her swirled black and ominous. *How many times can one area get hit by a tornado?*

Jenny quickly pulled the little nest from its precarious spot. The mother sparrow pecked her in the tender spot between thumb and forefinger. "Ow! You ingrate!" she chided the tiny bird. She settled the nest, with its inhabitants, into a crotch in a nearby tree.

Not a sparrow falls without my knowing.

Yes, Lord, Jenny replied.

She returned to her quest of opening the passenger-side door of Vanessa's damaged vehicle. It wasn't easy, but she wrestled the door open. Jenny eased herself down into the white leather bucket seat. "What are you doing, you idiot?" gasped Vanessa DuBois.

"I'm sitting down," Jenny replied dryly.

"Well, don't move anymore."

Jenny glanced down at the leg compartment on the driver's side. All she could see was the crushed dashboard and steering column. *Vanessa's legs are under that? How?* She wondered. Suddenly the fear dried up, replaced by pity. *She's going to lose her legs,* Jenny recognized.

Vanessa's face was pale, even paler than usual. Her lips were almost white. A thin line of sweat beaded on her upper lip. She turned hopeless eyes on Jenny.

"Do you know *why* I'm here, under this godforsaken tree?" she hissed.

"No." Jenny shook her head.

"Of course you don't," Vanessa whispered, turning away. "You wouldn't have tried to save my life if you knew."

"Knew what?" Jenny urged.

"I was coming back to finish the job. I was going to ram you head on. I couldn't figure out any other way to do it. You have stolen my horses *and* Daniel from me. You've outsmarted Marcus. *You* have everything, and I have nothing. Nothing!"

Chapter Seven

Jenny stared out the windshield into the broken mass of branches and pine needles. *What now, Lord?* she questioned. Anger, hatred, compassion, pity—all of these emotions raced down the back stretch of Jenny's soul. Which would win?

How weird to be sitting next to someone who has tried to kill you and herself just one hour ago.

I love her. Tell her.

Jenny fought the desire to roll her eyes. *You tell her,* she argued.

I have brought her to this place with you. I will reveal it to her, but you must say it.

Jenny fought to get her arms around that one. *So You protected me from her with this tree, but now you want me to tell her about You?*

Yes.

Why me?

Because Vanessa is right. You have everything, and she has nothing.

Now wait a minute. She has more money than . . . Daniel says she has more money than You.

She does not have Life. He who has the Son has Life. He who does not have the Son does not have Life. You have that Life. Now let it overflow as it should.

And what if I don't tell her? What happens then?

That is not for you to know.

"So, Vanessa," Jenny began, feeling really stupid. "Tell me about yourself."

Vanessa DuBois stared venomously at Jenny. "You may call me Mrs. DuBois," Vanessa retorted. "I worked very hard to become Mrs. DuBois."

"OK, Mrs. DuBois, tell me about yourself," Jenny persisted.

"Are you always so tenacious?" Vanessa hissed.

Jenny paused to think for a moment. "Yes, I think I am always tenacious, whatever that means."

Now Vanessa rolled her eyes. "Tenacious means persistent, never giving up."

"Oh," Jenny replied, smiling. "I'll take that as a compliment."

"Well, don't," the woman retorted. "I am the most tenacious person on the planet. I will *never* give up until that mare is dead."

Jenny felt a cold hard finger touch her heart, hardening it. "Mrs. DuBois," she cried angrily, "have you ever loved *anything*?"

Vanessa, who had puffed herself up with rage, deflated visibly. "No, never," she answered. She turned her head to gaze out the window.

Jenny noticed the quick, shallow breathing of the injured woman. *She looks like that little sparrow in the tree.*

She is like that bird, hopeless and helpless.

"I'm going to check on the horses," Jenny said, climbing out of the car and into the mass of pine needles. One pine needle poked her in the eye. "Ow!" she yelped. Her eye watered and complained for a minute and then settled down.

Jenny turned carefully and peered back into the Mercedes. Vanessa was still gazing the other way out the window.

"OK," Jenny muttered under her breath. "It's sure been nice chatting with you."

Jenny hadn't been away from the horses long, twenty minutes at the most. She checked the water buckets for both, and then went to rub Sunny's face.

Sunny nuzzled Jenny's hands, snuffling loudly.

"What? What do you smell, girl?" Jenny said.

The mare turned away suddenly and attended to her hay bag. Jenny stared at her open palms for a second. *She smelled Vanessa DuBois on my hands.*

Go back to the car. The thought was urgent.

Jenny hopped out of the trailer, closed the door, and hastened around the fallen tree.

She opened the driver's side door and looked. Vanessa's skin had a bluish tinge to it, and she was shaking violently. She groaned softly as Jenny opened the driver-side door. Vanessa's eyes opened briefly and sightlessly. Her thin blue lips parted. "I'm cold, so cold . . ."

Jenny's hardened heart melted. *She is dying*, Jenny realized. Suddenly all the anger stored up in Jenny's heart fell away like a huge weight. *Blankets! I need blankets.* The only blankets Jenny could think of were Sunny's blankets in the tack area of the trailer. She tore back around the fallen tree and flung the trailer tack door open. There was the wool cooler, the one she used after competition. She snatched it and ran.

She gently opened Vanessa's door again. Jenny doubled the blanket, and then quartered it. She placed it under Vanessa's chin and made sure it covered both arms. Then she dashed around to the passenger side and slid in. Vanessa was unconscious. Jenny pushed her seat all the way back, then reclined the back portion of the chair. She sat on the fully reclined seat back and carefully placed both arms around the woman's shaking body. After a couple of minutes Vanessa's shaking slowed a little. The wind gusted outside, shaking the car.

Talk to her.

Talk about what? Jenny's heart questioned.

Talk about Sunny and you and how I brought you together.

OK. I don't get it, but here goes . . .

"You know," Jenny started. "The way I met Sunny was amazing." She stared at Vanessa's face. No response. Nothing.

"Lord?" Jenny asked aloud. "Why am I doing this? She can't even hear me."

Keep talking, He replied to her heart.

"The way I met Sunny was amazing. I went to an auction with Kathy, you know, Kathy O'Riley. The auction was almost over, and this horse came out. She was nearly dead from starvation. Kathy said that they didn't usually sell those kinds of horses at that auction. Anyway, the meat man bought her for twenty-five dollars. Then he walked past Mom and me and he was hitting Sunny. Hitting her because she was too weak to walk fast, plus they were on gravel and she was lame from a terrible case of thrush." Jenny paused to stare at Vanessa's face. Nothing.

"Well, me and Mom—wait, Mom and I," she corrected herself. "Mom and I walked over to the meat man's trailer and bought Sunny for one hundred dollars. And it was my

money I'd earned at Sonrise Farm. Then Sunny collapsed in the parking lot and almost died, and Dr. Davis said she'd probably never be rideable. Oh! and this is funny. Kathy thought Sunny was ancient. Probably because she looked ancient."

Jenny sat up straight to look at the woman's face. Nothing. Jenny listened for a heart beat. It was faint but still there.

Tell her, He prodded.

"Well," Jenny continued, wrapping her arms around Vanessa again. "Then we had to figure out where we would keep her because Sonrise Farm doesn't do any boarding. They let us stay anyway. Sunny wouldn't let me out of her sight. The first time I went in to take a nap on a bed, Sunny flipped out. I had to sleep in her stall for a long while. I'd forgotten about that." Jenny smiled wryly at the memory made sweet with time and healing.

"Then," Jenny continued, "we had to see what kind of training she'd had, so Kathy's dad, Mr. O' Riley, got this cowboy friend of his to ride her for the first time. Whew, she was fast! So fast and strong that she ran away with him. She stopped, though, when I touched her. That cowboy told my dad to sell Sunny 'cause I'd never be able to handle her. Then, while they walked up to the barn, I hopped on her back, and she and I had the *best* ride!

"You know, Mrs. DuBois," Jenny murmured. "I'm thankful for you. If it weren't for you, I'd never have met Sunny. And if it weren't for you taking her away I'd never have *owned* Sunny, *and* I'd never have met Glory! All these things you meant for harm, God has turned to good for me. I would not be where I am now except for you."

Lord, that is amazing. I have never thought about Vanessa that way.

A glance at Vanessa's face told Jenny that they were fighting a losing battle. The woman was pale and cold. Suddenly Jenny really wanted her to live. And not just to live, but to have Life.

She's lost so much blood. Where is Daniel? Jenny wondered, staring at the clock on the wood-grain dashboard of the Mercedes. The clock still ran though the glass face was crushed. *He's been gone an hour.*

"Don't die, Mrs. DuBois," Jenny pleaded softly.

"Don't leave me," Vanessa moaned weakly. "Hold my hand."

"I will not leave you," Jenny assured her, taking the limp, cold hand in her own.

Then she heard the high-pitched squeal of a siren. Moments later, two paramedics jumped from the cab of an ambulance. They peeked in through Vanessa's side.

"How's she doin'?" a tall, dark man asked as he put the stethoscope to Vanessa's chest.

"I think she's dying," Jenny replied tearfully, staring at the young man's name badge. It said "Joe."

"Rick, get over here with some fluids!" Joe yelled. "And we're going to need the 'Jaws'[1] and a helicopter."

Daniel fought his way through the pine branches to get to the passenger side. He smiled tenderly at Jenny. His eyes were moist. "I knew I could count on you to do the good thing."

"What do you mean?" she asked.

"I knew you'd take care of her, no matter how you felt about her."

Jenny sat up, shoulders aching from the effort of keeping Vanessa warm.

"Do you think she'll die?" Jenny whispered. Just thinking it made the tears flow again.

"I don't know," Daniel answered. "She's hurt badly."

Joe started a little generator. The sound caused Vanessa to stir, but her eyes remained shut.

The two paramedics began cutting and removing the roof of the Mercedes Benz. Only when they began moving the dashboard did Vanessa open her eyes. Daniel got pushed aside as the vehicle opened like a tin can.

Above them, a helicopter started its descent to the road. The noise and wind swirling from the blades made Vanessa's eyes widen in terror.

"Joe, we've got her. Get the gurney," urged Rick.

The men placed a long backboard beside Vanessa and gently transferred her to it. She screamed as they moved her from the seat to the board. Her right leg dangled life-lessly.

Vanessa clutched Jenny's hand. "Please don't leave me," she begged. Jenny had to finally release her hand as they loaded her into the helicopter.

The two men worked over her for just a moment. Then Joe jumped out of the chopper and ran back to the ambulance.

"They'll take her to Loudoun Memorial," he shouted to Jenny and Daniel as he hopped into the ambulance. "It's got a trauma unit. We'll send someone to get you. We've got another call."

The chopper revved its engine and flew off. Rick flicked on the lights and siren, and the ambulance sped away.

Jenny and Daniel stared at each other for a moment then headed back toward the truck.

---

[1] Jaws of Life™ is a heavy-duty tool that cuts metal and seperates sections of it.

Chapter Eight

"Now what?" Jenny asked.

"We wait."

Jenny checked the horses once again. They both seemed calm. The filly dozed in the far corner of the trailer. Sunny pulled hay from the hay bag as though she'd lived in a trailer under a pine tree her whole life.

The storm had moved away, and the back road had become quiet. Jenny sat on the fender of the trailer. It was almost six in the evening, and hunger caused her stomach to complain loudly.

"Was that you or me?" Daniel asked, smiling tiredly.

They both looked up as a county sheriff's vehicle sped toward them. They waved as the officer slowed down. The sedan stopped, and a sheriff's deputy rolled down the window. "You OK?" she asked.

They nodded.

"I got a call from my dispatcher to pick up a couple of folks."

Daniel answered. "We *do* need a ride, but we've got two horses in the trailer. We can't leave them here."

"We've got a lot of storm damage everywhere, young man.

But I'll see what I can scrounge up for transport of two horses. Have a seat in here, and I'll get on the radio."

"Could someone call my parents and let them know we're all right?" Jenny inquired.

"Sure, honey," the deputy said with a smile. "What's your name?"

"Jenny Thomas," Jenny replied.

The deputy stared at her for a moment. "Jenny Thomas. Jenny Thomas, the world record puissance holder?"

"Yes," Daniel answered for her, grinning like a fool. "That Jenny Thomas."

"And are the horses in the trailer *your* horses, Miss Thomas?" Jenny nodded.

"And is Sunny one of the horses?" the police officer went on.

"Yes, ma'am," Jenny replied, grinning too. "It's Sunny and her filly in the trailer."

"And they're OK?" the woman asked, almost cringing at what the answer might be.

"A few scrapes, but they seem all right," Jenny replied.

"Miraculous!" the officer exclaimed. "My name is Ruth."

"Hi, Ruth," Jenny said, smiling.

"Climb in," said Ruth. "I know what to do."

They sped off down the road, siren blaring and lights flashing. The officer called a dispatcher on her radio. "Fran, I need Animal Control on Route 547, right where the tornado touched down. I've got two horses in a trailer. I want someone there until we can return with a working vehicle. We *do not* want anyone else running into that tree."

"Here is the phone, Miss Thomas," Officer Ruth said, handing it over her shoulder without looking back.

Jenny tried to recall her phone number. She felt dazed, and her thoughts were unclear.

"Daniel, what's my number?" she asked finally.

He gave her a look. "Are you sure you're all right?"

"I'm sure," she answered, rubbing just above her eyebrow. "Just tired."

Daniel recited the number, and she dialed.

"Hello?" Her mother's tight, worried voice answered.

"Mom, it's Jenny."

"Oh, Jenny! We've been so worried. Are you hurt? Where are you?"

"Um . . . we're fine. We are in the back of a police car, trying to find a trailer to bring the horses home."

"Are the horses all right?"

"I think so," Jenny replied slowly.

"We've seen so much tornado damage on the news. We called the equine hospital, and they told us you left three hours ago."

"We did leave, and we saw the tornado. It touched down right in front of us. It knocked a tree down, and we hit it with the truck. The same tree landed on Vanessa DuBois' car and crushed it. She's on her way to the hospital."

"Goodness, Jenny! Are you sure you're all right?"

"Yeah, Mom. I'm sure."

"Call me as soon as you know anything. Do you want your dad to come and help?"

"No, Mom," Jenny replied, stifling a yawn. "I think by the time he got here we'd be ready to go home."

"Well, be careful," Mrs. Thomas admonished. "We'll see you later this evening. And call me."

"I will," Jenny promised, smiling. As she closed the phone she murmured, "Boy, she's protective when she's pregnant."

"Who? Who's pregnant?'" Daniel inquired urgently.

"Oh, my mom."

"*Your* mom is expecting?"

"Yeah. She's due around Christmas. What's wrong with you?" she huffed.

"I don't know, I'm just used to you . . . you know, being the only one. I feel like you're my little sister, so now I'm going to have . . . I don't know. Someone new."

"Well," Jenny said, grinning. "Get used to the idea of someone new."

"Guess I'll have to," Daniel agreed, gazing out the window of the police car.

Soon the officer pulled into the driveway of a country house.

"Whose house is this, Ruth?" Jenny asked, looking at the tidy three-board fences around the pastures. Two tricolored paints grazed side by side in the far pasture behind the three-stall barn. An old palomino quarter-horse-type mare dozed under a large oak tree near the fence.

"This is my little my little herd," Ruth replied. "The big paint with the black tail is Bingo . . . I know, but that was his name when I got him. The young guy is Poncho, and the mare is an old school horse named Honey Pot.

"This is my house," Ruth continued. "I watched you and Sunny the night you broke the world record. That was the most exciting thing I've ever seen. I'm so thrilled to meet you. I'll just hook up my rig, and we'll get your girls where they need to go. Do you need anything? Halter? Leadrope?"

"Yeah, actually I need both," Jenny said. "Sunny's snapped."

"Here," Ruth replied, tossing Jenny a leather halter. "Take this one."

They climbed into Ruth's truck to rescue Sunny and Glory.

"You hungry?" Ruth asked as they passed a Dairy Queen.

Jenny had the *best* banana split she had ever eaten.

Chapter Nine

The horses were settled. Dr. Davis had come and checked them both. Sunny's knee was swollen but not seriously injured. The abrasion on her face would heal quickly.

"I shudder to think how this could have turned out, Jenny," Dr. Davis said grimly as he packed his bag.

"I know," she agreed. "I thought of that myself."

"Have a good night," he said as he doffed his hat. "I'll call Dr. Andrews in the morning and give him an update on Sunny."

"Thank you, Dr. Davis," she replied gratefully. "I'm so glad to be home."

Jenny dragged herself into the house. Warmth and delicious smells wafted over her, beckoning her to the kitchen.

After a gigantic dinner of spaghetti, Jenny headed for her room. "Oh, it's great to be home," Jenny sighed, falling backwards onto her bed. "After two weeks on a cot, or the floor, my bed feels like . . . heaven."

Jenny loved her room at Sonrise Farm Too. The view was amazing, with rolling pasture out the front window, Sunny's barn and paddock out the side, and woods out the back. Sometimes she saw a deer or a flock of wild turkeys.

But something was weighing on her mind as she rested.

Call and find out.

Jenny pried herself from the soft bed and made her way downstairs quietly. Her mother was already in bed after the excitement of the day.

"Dad?" she called softly. "Can we call the hospital where they took Mrs. DuBois?"

He looked up from his book, surprised. "Sure, sweetie," he replied. "Do you know where they took her?"

"Yes."

"Well, you don't need my help; just call information. They'll give you the number."

"I know," she choked, biting back tears. "I want to know, and I don't want to know."

"Know what?" he asked, looking confused.

"How *she* is," Jenny whispered. "*If* she made it."

"Ah," he nodded, understanding. "I'll call." He put a paper napkin in the book to hold his place and then rose from the easy chair.

She watched his face intently as he leaned against the kitchen counter, the phone to his ear, awaiting an answer.

"Hello, yes," he said and stood up straight. "We know someone who was taken to your emergency room this afternoon. We want to see how she is doing."

"Thank you." He covered the receiver with his hand. "She's transferring me to Emergency," he explained, relaxing back against the counter.

After a few moments Mr. Thomas straightened up once more. "Yes, hello. I'd like to get the status on a woman named Vanessa DuBois. She was brought to your emergency room this afternoon. No, we're not family. Yes . . . I'll hold."

He rolled his eyes. Jenny twirled her long hair around her finger nervously. *Lord, this is so weird. Why do I care about her?*

Because I care about her.

How can you care about her? She is so mean.

She has struggled to find Life from the world. She has failed. It always fails. She has come to the end of herself.

"Yes, I'm still here." Her father was talking again. "Yes, my daughter's name is Jenny . . . Really? . . . And when are visiting hours? . . . OK. Thank you for your help."

He slowly replaced the phone and turned toward Jenny. "She's lost her right leg just above the knee, and her left tibia was shattered. They had to put a plate in to hold it all together. They've got her in ICU, and, Jen, she's asking for *you*. The nurse said you could visit tomorrow . . . if you want to."

Jenny nodded her head. "I'd like to, Dad. Maybe Daniel will want to also."

Man, I hate hospitals, Jenny remembered as the sharp medicinal odors burned her nose. The last time she'd visited a hospital, she was visiting Patrick, Colton's son, and Daniel after the kidney transplant. She glanced at Daniel, amazed again that he would donate his kidney to Patrick. She had been so convinced he was a coward. *I wonder how he feels about being here,* she wondered.

Just the two of them were visiting Vanessa. Mrs. Thomas was struggling with morning sickness, and Mr. Thomas chose to stay with her.

Daniel's face was tight and pale. To Jenny he suddenly looked a little like Vanessa. She could see the family resemblance around the mouth and eyes. It made her shiver. She glanced at the rose she'd bought in the gift store downstairs. It was tired and shriveled from lack of water. *I wish I hadn't bothered*, she thought. *It just looks cheap.*

"Here it is, Room 617," Daniel whispered loudly. He walked through and held the door for Jenny. She walked in slowly, hiding the tired little rose behind her back.

Vanessa lay on the bed, eyes closed. She had oxygen tubes in her nostrils and an IV in the back of her hand. Her face was ashen, the skin tightly drawn over protruding cheek bones. *I never noticed how skinny she is*, Jenny thought, once again awash in pity. *She looks dead.* Jenny stood near the foot of the bed, afraid to move closer. Daniel moved, bumping the edge of the bed accidentally.

The movement woke Vanessa, and her eyes snapped open. She said nothing, just gazed warily at Jenny for several moments.

"So what are your plans?" Vanessa rasped weakly.

"What do you mean?" asked Jenny, confused by the abrupt question.

"Are you pressing charges?"

"Uh . . . no. I hadn't even thought about it," Jenny confessed. "I was worried about you and your . . . you know . . . your legs."

"Yeah, right. *You* are worried about *me* and my legs," Vanessa said sarcastically. "Why should you worry about me and my legs?"

"I don't know," Jenny said with a shrug. "I just am."

"Jenny kept you alive, Aunt Vanessa," Daniel said, louder than necessary.

"I know," the woman answered. "I just want to know *why*."

"Because!" Jenny began. She took a deep breath. "Because the Lord loves you, and He told me to. At least that's why I started."

"Puh!" Vanessa blew air through her tight white lips. "Love. What a strange word. It's just a word people use to squeeze what they can from you. It always ends. Badly."

She is wrong. I am Love.

"You're wrong, Mrs. DuBois," said Jenny softly. "Love is a person, the person of Jesus Christ. He is love." She brought the rose from behind her back. "This is for you. I know it's tired looking but . . ."

Vanessa stared at Jenny, eyes wide with surprise. She reached out with a shaking hand and took the rose. She studied it and then brought it to her nose for a moment. She stared at Jenny again with utter confusion.

"Daniel, leave us," Vanessa whispered, waving him away without looking at him. "I want to talk to this child alone."

Daniel threw Jenny a worried look, turned, and walked out.

"Nobody has ever given me flowers," Vanessa murmured, still cradling the rose. "In the car, while I was trapped, you kept me warm," she said. "I felt your arms around me, and I felt *safe*. No one has ever done anything like that for me. I don't understand you, Jenny Thomas. I have hated you and that horse. I have done everything in my power to kill that stupid mare, and you . . . you keep me alive and warm. I don't get it."

Jenny shrugged. "I don't really get it either, Mrs. DuBois. It's beyond me. All I know is that *He* told me to help you, and I did. In the process He showed me that all the things you've done actually helped me. Without you I never would have met Sunny or Glory."

"You asked me if I've ever loved anything," Vanessa said. "I lied to you in the car. I did love something. Twenty years ago when I was fifteen, I loved a little mare. She was a horse my dad's neighbors owned. Nothing special. They sold her to me because she got hurt and they didn't want to deal with it. It was a nasty kick wound, sliced right through the haunch muscle. The vet said she'd always have a scar and probably wouldn't be good for much. I took care of the wound, made

sure it was clean, didn't allow any proud flesh to form. And you know what?" Vanessa looked at Jenny, eyes gleaming. "It healed beautifully. She was sound as a dollar. The vet told me I was free to do whatever I wanted with her. She didn't even have a scar once the hair grew back.

"I *loved* that horse. I called her Honey. She had a funny little mark on her face, like a honey pot under her forelock." Vanessa's mouth twisted into a painful smile. "She was so brave, so sweet. She did anything I asked." Vanessa's eyes softened as she remembered.

"I started showing her, and we cleaned up wherever we went. One day we were at a show, and some guy came up and offered my dad a wad of cash for Honey. My dad took it." She shook her head, her eyes glistening with pain. "I still can't believe he did it. Sold her right out from under me. I came out of my class on cloud nine and had to hand my sweet mare to some girl I'd never seen before."

Vanessa stared at the IV line in the back of her hand. A single tear dropped. She rubbed it away as though it was burning the spot it touched.

"That girl took her in the last class," she continued in a soft, faraway voice. "Honey wasn't used to rough riding, and she balked at a jump. The girl beat her. My sweet mare. They beat her. Then they loaded her up and took her away. I never saw her again. My dad told me to grow up and stop bawling. So I did. He never saw me cry again. And I vowed to never love anything like that. It's not worth the pain."

Vanessa stared at Jenny, daring her to say something cruel.

Jenny drew in a deep breath to make up for the ones she hadn't taken during Vanessa's story. She sat carefully on the edge of Vanessa's hospital bed. "I'm so sorry your dad did that. I can't imagine how that must have felt."

How would *I feel if Dad sold Sunny? Mad . . . and then so sad. For myself and Sunny.*

"Aren't you afraid your love for Sunny won't last?" Vanessa asked, looking softer. "What if she dies or your dad sells her?"

"My dad wouldn't do that. And if she dies I'll be heart-broken. But even if that happens, it is worth the pain of loving her."

Vanessa sighed. "I've looked for love in horses, in my dad, in money, in my husband. They've all left me. There is nothing. I'm tired. *I'm* ready to die and get it over with. Will you help me?"

"No," Jenny responded quietly. "But I can help you find Life."

"I told you. I've tried it all. Nothing works."

"Have you tried Jesus?" Jenny probed gently.

"Please, don't patronize me." Vanessa's hard shell returned instantly. "I'm *not* going to get all religious. That's for people who are too weak to deal with their problems."

"I see," Jenny replied sweetly. "So how is it going, you know, *you* dealing with your problems?"

Vanessa fingered the rose she was still clutching. "Not so well," she finally admitted.

"And," Jenny continued, "it's not about religion. It's a relationship. A relationship with a Man who is also God. A Man who loves you so much, He'd rather die than be without you. He conquered death so we could have Life. So *you,* Mrs. DuBois, could have Life."

"I've never heard that before," Vanessa said softly. "And call me Vanessa. It *is* true that I worked hard to become 'Mrs. DuBois,' but all it's bought me is pain. I thought Luc would be the answer to all my problems. He was rich, hand-some, and *so* charming. He told me he wanted to take care of me . . . to give me the moon if I wanted it. He mentioned one

day that his 'dream wife' would have blond hair. I've been blond ever since. That was a test, I guess. To see if I would jump through the hoops.

"I'd have done anything to get him to marry me. We had a huge wedding in Paris, where he grew up, and we settled here in Virginia. I had never been out of the state of California. I was so tired of scraping by; I had done it my whole life. My dad always told me to marry rich. And I did. You know what's funny? My dad wouldn't even come to my wedding. Nope. I offered to fly him and everything."

"So what happened?" Jenny asked gently.

"We were married for two years. Luc wanted a large family with lots of kids. After a year it became clear that I couldn't have children. So he left me. The last I heard, he'd married a beautiful Swedish girl and they had three kids.

"He gave me the farm here in Virginia and plenty of money. I *should* be over it by now. It was ten years ago . . . why can't I get over it?"

Jenny could only shrug helplessly.

A nurse breezed in. "Time for a blood pressure and temp check," she said. "How are we doing today, Mrs. DuBois? Are you ready for some more pain medication?"

Vanessa pushed herself upright. "Yeah, maybe," she grimaced. "It's weird. I know my foot is gone but it still hurts."

"That's called phantom pain, Mrs. DuBois. It's normal," the nurse explained. To Jenny she said, "Morning visiting hours are over in fifteen minutes, young lady, so please finish up. You may come back this evening. Hours are six to eight."

"I'll go," Jenny whispered.

"Can you come back tomorrow?" Vanessa asked.

"I'll try," Jenny promised.

Chapter Ten

"You didn't buy it? Did you?" Daniel asked, sounding genuinely concerned, as he drove them home from the hospital.

"Yes, Daniel. I really think she's different," Jenny replied.

"Jenny," he huffed. "She's on morphine for pain, so she's loopy from that, *plus,* how do you think she gets people to do what she wants? I helped her starve the horses I now love, because she seemed like this helpless, pathetic thing that the whole world was against. She has had some hard knocks. I feel sorry for her, and in a weird way I love her. But she's scary. Very scary. She's a master manipulator. Just like her dad."

"Her dad is your grandpa," Jenny said slowly, as the thought dawned on her. "Did you ever know him?"

"Yeah, I knew him all right. He came to live with us in California. He didn't stay very long. He's kind of a loud, angry man, if you know what I mean. He and my dad used to get into it. One day they got so loud, my mom called the cops. Grandpa took off before the police got there. I've never seen him since. And good riddance."

"What about the rest of your family, out there in California? Do you miss them?" Jenny questioned.

"Not enough to go back," Daniel said. "My time with Colton and Patrick at Cedar Creek has shown me what family *should* be like. It's hard to want to go back to screaming and punching."

"Punching?" Jenny gasped. "*Punching?*"

"A couple times," Daniel said, shrugging nonchalantly. "No biggie."

Uncomfortable silence hung in the air like a cloud. *Grandpa and Daddy, shouting and hitting.* No matter how hard she tried, she couldn't imagine it.

Lord, Jenny's heart cried. *How can Daniel or Vanessa have a good picture of You, when all they know is punching and screaming?*

I will heal their hearts.

How?

Through you.

Daniel was right. Fury did look fabulous. His eyes were bright but soft and calm. He was just the right weight, filled out and athletic. Daniel haltered the young stallion and then led him on a long lead to the ring. He bent the horse's head toward him and untied the rope halter. Fury stuck to him like glue. Then, with a look and a finger shake from Daniel, Fury backed up and waited, watching Daniel the way a border collie watches sheep, with total concentration. Daniel sent him to the left at a brisk trot.

Jenny's heart pounded like Fury's hooves. *He's magnificent,* she thought. She couldn't think of a better word to describe him. *"Gorgeous" is overused. "Cute" just doesn't do it. "Majestic" . . . that works.*

Fury floated around Daniel in a small circle, keeping Daniel at the center. With one glance, Daniel invited the big horse to turn and come in. Fury threw his hindquarters out with an exuberant buck and came in immediately. He licked his lips and lowered his head for Daniel to rub.

"Daniel," Jenny choked, astounded, "he's wonderful. He looks . . . amazing."

"Thank you." Daniel sighed with satisfaction. "Working with this horse has been the highlight of my life. Thank you for the chance, Jen. I *know* you must have been worried after all I did before."

She gazed back at him. "I *was* worried, Daniel, and I'm so sorry."

"It's all right," he said, smiling. "You gave me a chance, and I can't tell you what that means to me." Daniel slipped the halter back on Fury's head and handed Jenny the lead rope. "He's yours, Jenny. I need to get back to Cedar Creek."

Daniel stroked Fury's powerful neck. The horse leaned into his caress like a cat.

Daniel's eyes welled up. "I'm going to miss you, boy." His voice cracked.

Then he turned quickly and started toward his truck.

He belongs with Daniel.

And Jenny *knew* it was true.

"Daniel! Wait!" Jenny called.

Daniel stopped but didn't turn around. Jenny slipped between the rails of the ring and jogged toward him. "Here," she said firmly, handing him the rope. "Here is the lead rope for *your* horse."

He said nothing, just stared at her, as tears began to flow.

They warmed up leftover food from the night before. "Can I call Colton?" Daniel asked. "I can't wait to tell him about Fury."

"Sure," Jenny said, smiling, as she opened the microwave and traded plates. She put Daniel's plate on the table. "Ouch," she exclaimed, popping her thumb in her mouth. "That sauce is hot!"

Mrs. Thomas wandered into the kitchen. "What's cooking?" she asked hopefully.

"Spaghetti. You want some?" Jenny asked. "There's plenty."

"I shouldn't," Mrs. Thomas said in a less-than-convinced tone.

"Oh, come on, Mom. You need your strength. You're eating for two now."

Jenny's mother rubbed her growing tummy thoughtfully. "I just don't want to gain as much weight as I did when I had you."

"Sit. I'll get you some," Jenny insisted.

"Thank you, sweetie," Mrs. Thomas sighed, sinking into the kitchen chair.

Jenny heard Daniel say into the phone, "I'll see you later tonight."

"Wait!" she shrieked. "I want to talk to Colton!"

Daniel handed her the phone.

"Colton! How are you?" she squealed joyfully.

"I am well." Jenny could hear the warm grin in his voice. "I am very proud of you, young lady. Giving Fury to Daniel. Whew, that's neat."

"You won't believe the conversation I had with Daniel's aunt yesterday," Jenny gushed. "She told me about this horse she loved and how her dad sold the mare out from under her at a show! She was really talking to me. She is *different*. Daniel says I'm nuts to believe a word she says but . . . I want to believe her. I want her to be different, for her sake as well as mine."

"Why don't you invite her to church when she's released from the hospital?" Colton suggested.

"Great idea!" Jenny agreed.

"And I would keep talking to her, if you can. Just be careful, Jenny. Daniel knows her better than you do."

"I will," Jenny promised. "Thank you, Colton."

"Thank you, Jennifer Lynne," he replied. "I am still blown away by your giving Fury to Daniel. You are awesome!"

"It was God's idea," she replied. "I just did what He said."

"I know . . . that's what is so wonderful. He asks and then you do it. Very unusual."

"Hmm," Jenny mused. "I think that's your fault, Colton."

"Really?" he said. "How's that?"

"Well, *you're* the one who showed me the picture of Jesus' relationship with me, and my relationship with Sunny. I imagine what *I* want Sunny to do when I ask her. Do I want her to think about it and then do what makes sense to her, or do I want her to trust me and do what I ask even if it seems strange to her? I love Sunny. I will never ask her to do something she shouldn't do. I know Jesus loves me even more."

"I'll say it again," Colton breathed. "Jennifer Lynne. You are something else. Thank you for that. Love you, girl. Let me know what happens with Mrs. DuBois."

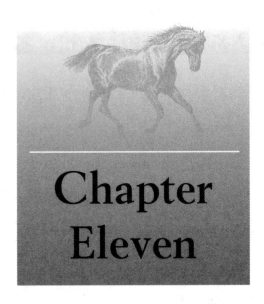

Chapter Eleven

I think she's changed since yesterday, Jenny marveled, watching Glory romp in circles around Sunny. Every day the filly looked bigger, more coordinated, more *alive*. And every day Sunny looked better. She hardly dragged her hind toes anymore, a good sign her nerves were recuperating.

Jenny slipped through the rails and approached the filly. She walked slowly, and Sunny whickered and walked sedately to meet her.

"Hi, Sunny," Jenny said, smiling as she hugged the mare's neck. Sunny wrapped her long neck around Jenny in response. Glory galloped away, squealing and bucking. "Whoa, Glory," Jenny said with a laugh. "You're gonna fall over. Your legs are everywhere!"

The filly stayed up, careening around the pasture like a wild thing. She finally grew tired of chasing the wind and trotted back to Sunny and Jenny. She bumped her nose into Sunny's udder and started nursing, her little blond tail flipping back and forth in delight.

Thank you, Lord, Jenny's heart cried.

Thank you, He replied.

For what? Jenny asked, mystified.

For expressing My love to Vanessa and to Daniel.

Jenny stayed several hours, brushing the "girls" and play-ing with them. At about 3:30 in the afternoon, Jenny and Glory curled up together under a shady oak tree. The filly's body was now longer than Jenny. Sunny dozed in the shade, standing up, one hind leg cocked.

From far away Jenny heard the barn phone ring. *Someone else will get it*, she thought lazily. The phone continued to ring. *Tenacious,* she thought, smiling to herself and slowly rising from the soft grass. The filly raised her head for a moment and then flopped back down to continue her nap. Sunny shifted her weight to the other side, cocking the other hind leg.

"Sonrise Farm Too," Jenny yawned into the phone.

"May I speak to Mrs. Thomas?" the voice requested.

Jenny glanced at the house. "She's inside, and I'm in the barn. Can you hold for a moment? I'll go find her."

I wonder why Mom didn't answer, Jenny mused as she jogged the short distance to the house.

"Mom," she yelled. "Telephone for you!"

No one answered.

Check the bedroom.

And there she was, unconscious on the floor.

"Mom!" Jenny screamed.

There was no response.

Jenny picked up the phone to dial 911. "Hello, Mrs. Thomas?" the voice asked.

"No," Jenny blurted, "I need to hang up and call 911. She's lying on the floor. Oh, . . . I can't call. The phone in the barn is off the hook!"

"Stay calm," said the voice. "This is Loudoun Memorial Hospital. I was calling to give an update on Mrs. DuBois. I'll call 911 for you. What is your address?"

Jenny gave her the address and explained the long driveway. "You'll have to go past the big yellow house. Our farm is tucked in a grove of trees. Our sign says 'Sonrise Farm Too.'"

"I'm calling them now," the nurse replied. "You stay on the phone with me. Does your mother have a pulse?"

"Yes," Jenny said as she finally exhaled. "And she's breathing."

"Good," said the nurse. "Stay right there and watch. Do you know CPR?"

"Yes," Jenny replied.

"Great," the nurse said. "Someone should be there soon."

Jenny was at Loudoun Memorial Hospital for the second time that day. She sat in the waiting room, feeling frustrated and upset. Her father arrived a half hour later, breathless. "What's going on?" he asked, giving Jenny a hug.

"I don't know, Daddy," she replied, squeezing him hard around the middle. "They still haven't told me anything."

"Miss Thomas," a female doctor called.

"How is she?" Mr. Thomas questioned intently.

"She seems to be fine. We've admitted her, and she's in a room where we can watch her. It may have just been low blood sugar. We are still running tests. But she's awake and asking for you. Go down the hall to the second room on the left."

The two speed-walked down the hall to the room.

"Mom!" Jenny cried in utter relief. "You scared me to death!"

"I'm sorry, Jenny. Hi, Mike. I don't know what happened. I was taking a little nap and the phone rang. I got up to answer it, and that's the last thing I remember."

Mr. Thomas pulled up a chair and sat holding his wife's hand in his. "I'm just glad you're all right."

"They want to keep me overnight," Mrs. Thomas said.

"I think *that* is a good idea," Mr. Thomas answered. "We don't want any repeats of last time."

"What last time?" Jenny asked. "What are you talking about?"

Mr. Thomas glanced at his wife, who nodded back at him. "Your mom lost a baby once. You were two years old, Jenny. We almost lost your mom in the process."

"Why didn't you tell me?" Jenny gasped.

"Well, sweetheart," her mother said thoughtfully, "you were too young to understand at the time, and then, I don't know . . . It never came up. Your dad and I wanted more children, and it just didn't happen until now."

"Wow, Mom. I had no idea. Are you afraid?"

"No, Jenny, I'm excited. We'll see what the Lord has in store for this little one."

The doctor sauntered in, reading a chart as she went. She looked up at the three waiting faces. "Some of the tests are back. It looks like you are anemic."

"So . . . what does that mean?" Mr. Thomas asked.

"Iron supplements," the doctor answered with a quick smile. "I'll write a prescription. We'll keep her overnight, just as a precaution, but I'm almost positive she can go home tomorrow."

"Whew!" Mr. Thomas breathed. "I felt a few gray hairs pop out on that one," he said, smiling.

"Mom, do you mind if I go visit Vanessa?" Jenny asked.

"No, you go right ahead. I'll wait here."

"Very funny, Mom," Jenny said, smiling.

Jenny found the door to Vanessa's room closed. She headed for the nurse's station.

"Hi," she greeted. A young male nurse looked up from the computer. "Can I help you?" he said gruffly.

"Yes, I'd like to visit Vanessa DuBois in room 617, but the door is closed."

"Yup, she's getting fitted for prosthesis."

"What's a pross, proth, . . . what is that?" Jenny asked.

"It's a fake leg. She'll get an initial fitting now, and as soon as her stump heals, she'll go to rehab. The sooner she's up and about, the better."

"When will she be able to have visitors?" Jenny inquired.

"Are you immediate family?" he asked.

"No. I'm not family, just a . . . friend." *That sounds weird,* she thought. *I never imagined I might be a friend to Vanessa DuBois. Maybe acquaintance is the right word.*

You are the best friend Vanessa ever had.

"Let me check," the nurse replied.

He returned in a moment. "You can go in. The prosthesis is fitted, and she could use a friend right now."

Vanessa was crying. Her ice-blue eyes were swollen and red. "It's gone," she sobbed, staring at the outline of her stub under the sheet. "It's really gone. I don't think I had focused on it before. How am I going to walk, or drive or . . . ride? What am I going to do? I have no 'support system.' Without that I have to *live* in at rehab for two months."

Jenny poured some water into a plastic cup. She handed it to Vanessa.

"I'd rather die than give up my independence," Vanessa said passionately.

"I'll help you," Jenny promised. "And Daniel will help."

"We'll see," Vanessa huffed. "I'm pretty sure he hates me."

"My mom is here," Jenny said, changing the subject.

"Why?"

"She's expecting, and she fainted today. They think she's just anemic, but it sure scared us."

"I'd like to meet your mom," Vanessa said softly.

"You have," Jenny replied, surprised. "When you came to Sonrise Farm to claim Sunny."

"You're right. I had forgotten. It seems so long ago."

"Maybe I can bring her up later," Jenny suggested. "I'm sure she'd like to meet you too."

"I never knew my mom," Vanessa whispered. "She died when I was five."

When she asked about being Vanessa's support system, Jenny was shocked by the finality of her father's answer.

"No, Jenny, Vanessa cannot live with us. Your mother needs *less* work, not more. You and I need to take care of Mom. Let Daniel help his aunt."

"But Dad!" Jenny blurted. "I'm her only hope."

Mr. Thomas smiled lovingly. "No, Jen. You are not her only hope. Jesus is our only hope. Your mom and I prayed about this while you visited Vanessa. He told me clearly that I'm to look after Mom right now."

"Why didn't He tell me?" Jenny sniffled.

"Did you ask?" Mr. Thomas asked pointedly.

"No, I just assumed—"

"Ah. Well, give me a hug. I could sure use one."

She squeezed as though she'd never let go.

Chapter Twelve

"Daniel, she needs you. She has no one else," Jenny pleaded into the phone. "My mom needs to take it easy, and I'll have my hands full helping Mom."

"It's not *my* fault she alienates everyone around her," Daniel growled back.

"Just ask Colton. I know he'll say yes."

"I don't want to ask Colton. I don't want her here. This is my place. This is my peace. She ruins everything she touches."

"What if she just needs a chance, Daniel? Like you. You needed me to give you a chance with Fury. I'm so glad I did!"

"How do you know she's for real this time?" Daniel asked.

"Because God is telling me," she responded.

"All right," he said, defeated. "I'll ask Colton if she can stay here for a while. But just until her rehab is over. As soon as she can drive and walk, she's outta here."

"Let me know what Colton says."

A week later, Vanessa DuBois left the hospital. She was headed for Cedar Creek with Colton and Daniel. No one seemed happy with the idea except Colton. As he and Jenny spoke before they left, he seemed genuinely pleased with the whole situation.

"I think this will be great, Jen," he chortled. "I see real hope for restoration."

"What do you mean?" Jenny asked.

"Well, you and Daniel can forgive Vanessa without her permission or knowledge, but you can't have restoration without Vanessa getting involved. I see this as an opportunity for the Lord to replace the years the locusts have eaten."

"Huh?" Jenny said.

"The restoration of Israel. Go home and read the book of Joel, chapter two, verse twenty-five. It was God's promise to His people that He would make things like new."

"I will read it," Jenny promised with a nod. "Have a good trip, Colton." She hugged him around the neck. "I miss you and Daniel, and I think I'm even going to miss Vanessa."

As they pulled away from the hospital in Colton's big dually, Jenny waved until she couldn't see them anymore.

The thought of Honey, Vanessa's lost horse, continued to haunt Jenny. *How could a loving dad do that to his child?* she thought.

Vanessa has learned that love is not about what you take. Taking is the opposite of true love.

"Dad?" Jenny said as she fastened her seatbelt to go home.

"Yes," he replied, smiling.

"Where is the book of Joel in the Bible? I've never heard of it."

"It's near the end of the Old Testament. Why?"

"I'm supposed to look up a verse about locusts eating something."

He laughed aloud. "Colton is my guess for that assignment."

Lying in bed that evening, Jenny found Joel 2:25, read it through, and tried to make sense of it.

" 'I will repay you for the years the locusts have eaten,' " it said.

Restoration. She liked the sound of it. Turning out the light, she closed her eyes and was soon asleep.

She dreamed of a young Vanessa riding a pretty palomino mare named Honey.

"Sun-ny. Glo-ry. Break-fast," Jenny called, splitting the words in the middle. Glory careened around the corner while Sunny walked sedately behind. "You are still dragging that toe just a little, aren't you, girl?" she said to Sunny. The filly was beginning to eat grain from her own little bucket. She dipped her delicate muzzle into the bucket, and Jenny heard the "crunch, crunch, crunch" of sweet feed.

Jenny rubbed Sunny's itchy spot, the one on her neck just above the shoulder. The mare's upper lip tightened, giving her a funny look. She stretched out her neck like a giraffe. Jenny stopped rubbing, and Sunny sighed and began eating her grain.

"I wonder whatever happened to Honey with the funny little honey pot on her head," Jenny said to Sunny. "And *you* were supposed to be just like Honey, but you weren't. You were too different."

"Who are you talking to?" a voice said.

Jenny inhaled a tiny scream and then held her hand over her pounding heart as she turned to Kathy. "Where did you come from? You scared me to death!" she exclaimed, resting a moment on the fence rail.

"Well, who *are* you talking to?" Kathy repeated.

"I was talking to Sunny about Vanessa and Vanessa's horse named Honey. Kathy, twenty years ago, Vanessa's dad sold her horse while Vanessa was riding in a class."

"Wait," Kathy sputtered. "You mean he sold the horse while she was in the class?"

"Yeah!" Jenny answered. "She walks out of the class and has to hand over *her* horse, that she bought with her own money, to some girl she's never seen before. Then *that* girl tried to take Honey in a class and beat her when she wouldn't jump. Poor Vanessa had to watch the whole thing." Jenny sighed heavily. "I don't know why, but I just keep thinking about it."

"That's weird," Kathy said, shaking her head. "I just saw a halter with the name Honey Pot. It's hanging in the barn. It's a halter I've never seen before."

"Show me," Jenny said, heading toward Sonrise Farm's jumper barn.

"No, it's in your barn. I'll show you."

The halter was hanging on a hook outside Sunny's stall. It was a well-oiled leather halter with a brass plate inscribed with the name Honey Pot.

"Weird," Jenny said, feeling a little strange.

"I came to the house first to find you," Kathy explained. "Your mom said you were out here feeding the 'girls.' I walked by Sunny's stall and noticed it. It's a nice halter. Where did it come from?"

"I don't know," Jenny replied, shaking her head.

"It's got a nice lead rope too," Kathy said, fingering the soft, heavy rope.

"The lead rope!" Jenny said suddenly. "Sunny's lead and halter broke in the crash. This must belong to Ruth, the police officer who gave us a ride home. I remember she said I could use her halter. I must have forgotten to give it back.

And . . ." Suddenly Jenny had goose bumps. "She has an old mare named Honey!"

The two ran to Kathy's truck, jumped in, and drove toward Ashland and Ruth's farm.

"I can't stand it!" Jenny said. "What if it really is the same Honey? What will we do?"

"It's probably not the same horse, Jen," Kathy warned. "But if it is, just tell the woman the story. Maybe she'll sell her to you. At the very least you can tell Vanessa where Honey is—if it's even the same horse."

Jenny stared at the halter in her hands. It didn't look twenty years old. *This is not the same horse. It couldn't be . . . after all these years.*

Just see.

They entered the driveway of Officer Ruth's farm. The old mare was standing under the same tree she'd been under when Jenny first saw her. Her back looked a little swayed, but not bad; she was a little ribby, but that wasn't bad either. She desperately needed brushing, and her feet were long. *Not too bad . . . considering*, Jenny thought.

Kathy knocked on the front door. Ruth came out and greeted them warmly, her dark brown eyes twinkling. "So, you stole my halter, did you?" she teased, looking at what Jenny was holding in her hands. "I think that's petty larceny."

"Thank you for all your help that day," Jenny said with a smile, feeling a little uncomfortable. "Could we go look at your old mare?"

Ruth's eyes widened for a moment. "Uh, sure. But why?"

"I'll tell you on the way," Jenny said.

As they walked down to the pasture, Jenny explained to Ruth why she wanted check out Honey Pot's face. She walked up to the horse, pulled back the forelock, and saw a perfect honey pot!

"Can I buy her from you?" Jenny begged. "I'd love to give her back to my friend."

"You can have her," Ruth said, smiling wide. "She's been standing in my field for the last five years. I bought her as a companion for my Poncho, but then I got Bingo. I didn't have the heart to sell her. Some of the neighbor kids play around on her, and she's a great baby-sitter. I'd be thrilled to think she was with you."

"Perfect!" Jenny blurted, feeling almost dizzy. *Lord, you are so fun!* Her spirit sang.

I love you, Jennifer Lynne, He sang back.

She smiled.

Chapter Thirteen

"So how is Vanessa doing?" Jenny asked Colton over the phone.

"Very well," he replied. "She's over the depression, and she's starting to lean some weight on the prosthesis. Hey! She and Daniel came to church last week!"

"You're kidding," Jenny said. "How did you get her there?"

"It's a funny thing," he replied, chuckling low. "When you can't walk or do anything for yourself, if the rest of the house goes to church, you have to go."

"Well," Jenny urged, "how was it?"

"Pastor is doing a series on forgiveness and redemption. Amazing coincidence, don't you think? And the ladies ate her up. She was overwhelmed, I think, by the love."

Jenny smiled.

"Vanessa could use some female company, Jen. Poor thing—surrounded by men. Can you come visit?"

"I think it will be a month or two. Mom is feeling a little better, but the doc says it takes a couple months. I have a surprise for Vanessa," Jenny said with a giggle.

"Really?" Colton said. "Do tell."

"No," she replied in a teasing tone. "You can wait too."

"Come on, Jenny," he cajoled. "I'm the one who helped you win the world's record puissance. That's the least you can do."

Jenny grinned. "All right. But it is a *secret!*"

"Yes, ma'am," he barked.

Jenny stood balanced on a bucket in Sunny's stall, peeking through the back window. Every morning she turned Sunny out and watched through the window as the mare circled the spot where she *wanted* to roll. Sunny hadn't had a good roll or slept on the ground since the foaling. Jenny watched Sunny do the little circle ritual every day. Every day she prayed it would happen.

The big mare bent her right knee and started to go down. Then she popped back up. She circled some more, head cocked, left ear down, focusing on the ground.

Come on, Sunny, you can do it, Jenny thought.

The mare went to both knees the second time. Jenny held her breath. *This is it!*

Sunny jumped back up, circled, and began the process again. This time she got all the way down on her right side but didn't roll. Instead, she leapt up immediately.

What on earth is she doing? Jenny wondered.

The fourth time Sunny went down, she rolled and rolled. She lay flat, rubbing her long neck back and forth in the dirt on both sides. The big mare grunted with pleasure as she scratched the itchy spots that had gone unscratched for months. Then, when every itchy place was thoroughly caked in wet dirt, Sunny jumped up, launching skyward, bucking and squealing with joy.

Glory watched her mama for a second and then took off after her, little tail high in the air, neighing with delight.

Jenny watched her mare and filly romp through her joy-filled tears.

A word blew in on the rustling breeze.

Restoration.

Jenny braided silk flowers into Honey's freshly washed mane. She knotted the mare's forelock so that the honey-pot marking was visible. She brushed the mare's wide back, now nicely round, one last time then walked her onto the trailer.

"She looks great, Jen!" Kathy said. "Whatever you've been feeding her has sure made her fill out."

Jenny smiled. "Do you think the flowers in her mane are too much?"

"She looks great. I wouldn't worry about a thing."

"I think she'll knock Vanessa's socks off." *Or sock off,* Jenny thought, remembering the amputation. *I'll have to watch what I say.*

Kathy nodded.

They loaded Sunny and Glory and were off to Cedar Creek.

Kathy's truck pulled up and parked under the Cedar Creek sign. Jenny peered out and spied a young, dark-haired woman sitting in a lawn chair next to Patrick. They appeared to be talking intently. Colton and Daniel were putting up hay in the barn.

Maybe that's Patrick's girlfriend? Jenny considered. *Where is Vanessa?*

She and Kathy climbed out of the truck just as her father and mother pulled up in their station wagon. Colton looked up and spied them. "Hello!" he called as he ran toward them.

"Jenny, Kathy, how are you?" He embraced them both warmly. "Mike and Judy, so glad you could make it." He kissed

Mrs. Thomas on the cheek, then stood back to admire her rounded tummy. "You look radiant!" he remarked.

She smiled up at him, "Thank you, Colton."

"Wow, it's like old times!" he said. "Everyone's here."

"Who is that sitting with Patrick?" Jenny inquired.

"That's Vanessa. Come see her," Colton said with a smile.

Jenny could not believe her eyes. The harsh bleach-blond hair was gone, and Vanessa's face had filled out—she just looked different. *She looks peaceful*, Jenny realized. *And so pretty*.

"Hi, you guys," Vanessa yelled from across the yard.

Jenny jogged over. "I can't believe how different you look," she exclaimed.

"Oh, the hair. Do you like it? I've returned to my natural state."

"You look beautiful!"

A commotion from the trailer reminded Jenny of her lovely errand. "Vanessa, I have a surprise for you."

"Really?"

"Really." She ran back and opened the trailer door.

Vanessa sat quietly gazing up at Colton as Jenny approached with the mare. Honey Pot suddenly pricked up her ears, nickering loudly in Vanessa's direction.

Colton stopped talking and turned his eyes on the old mare. He nodded for Vanessa to do the same. She smiled and turned to see.

The smile disappeared as her jaw dropped. She blinked and then sat forward, almost squinting. The closer Jenny got, the more delighted she became at Vanessa's expression.

Finally, Jenny and the mare came close to her. Honey nudged Vanessa with her nose. Vanessa reached out her trembling hand to stroke the mare's face. She touched gently as though the horse might vanish.

"Honey!" she cried, struggling to stand.

Colton reached out and lifted Vanessa out of the chair in his arms, and placed her on the mare's back. Vanessa slid forward, hugging Honey's neck ferociously, tears drenching the mare's mane. "I looked for you forever. I can't believe you've come back to me now. Thank you, Jenny. I can't tell you what this means to me."

"You should thank Him. It was a God thing for sure."

"Welcome home, Honey," Colton said, smiling and stroking the mare's neck. "And welcome home, honey," he said to Vanessa quietly. Vanessa beamed down at him from her perch. The mare released a huge sigh.

They ate Chinese that night. Jenny tried the chopsticks, to no avail. "Didn't we have lo-mein the *last* time we were at your house?" Jenny asked pointedly.

"Hey, we are a bunch of bachelors," Colton replied playfully. "Or we were before the lovely Vanessa came along." He reached out and squeezed Vanessa's hand.

Jenny couldn't miss the look Vanessa gave Colton. It was *love*.

"Chinese food," Colton continued, "*is* the stuff of life. The alternative is not pretty. I can, and have, melted cast-iron pans in the process of cooking."

Jenny couldn't stop staring at the joined hands on the table.

"All right, I was going to wait, but I think *now* is the time," Colton said. He stood up, cleared his throat, and gazed at Vanessa for a moment. "Vanessa and I are getting married."

Chapter Fourteen

"What?" Jenny screeched and then choked, "Married?"

"Yep," he said, grinning. "I knew you'd be thrilled, Jen," he teased. "November 27th is the big day. I've reserved the preacher and everything. You all are invited."

Jenny stared at Daniel with open hands. Daniel shook his head, grinning.

"That's Thanksgiving!" Jenny announced, not looking at Vanessa. "How can you get married on Thanksgiving?"

"Well," Colton began, "first you call a preacher, and then you ask him to come to your place of marriage—"

"No! I don't mean literally," Jenny huffed.

"Well, I think the best thing to do is have everyone arrive on Wednesday. Vanessa is already living in the cottage next to Daniel's. Patrick can move in with Dan for a couple days. Kathy, your parents can take the cottage on the far side of Vanessa's, and Kathy, if *you* don't mind sharing a room with Jenny, I think we'll all fit!"

"I can handle sharing a room," Kathy said with a smile. She winked at Jenny. "And we thought *we* had a surprise."

Why am I not happy about this? Jenny pondered. *What if she's up to something?*

Colton's church was not close by, but then, nothing was close by his place. He lived far out in the boonies.

Colton plucked Vanessa out of her wheelchair as though she were a child. Vanessa threw her arms around his neck and smiled, her face glowing.

He placed her gently in the front seat of his dually truck and then folded the wheelchair and tucked it in the back of his truck. Jenny and Kathy climbed into the back seat of the crew cab, while Jenny's parents followed in the station wagon.

Daniel and Patrick brought up the rear of the convoy in Colton's old, beat-up Toyota.

The church was small and warm. Colton carried Vanessa up the stairs and placed her gently in the wheelchair. The congregation gathered around her, greeting and hugging and loving her.

"Vanessa, dear," a sweet, elderly lady in a big pink hat chirped. "Do you think you could come to our Ladies' Tea this weekend if I picked you up?"

Vanessa smiled beautifully. "I'd *love* to, Rosemary," she said, blushing. She *looked* as though she would love to.

Lord, Jenny's heart complained, *why am I so . . . unhappy about Vanessa's engagement to Colton?*

She didn't hear an answer. Her thoughts wandered. *What is she up to?*

"Forgiveness," the pastor said loudly.

Jenny sat up straighter, trying to focus on his words.

"Forgiveness is a one-way street. What I mean by that is, you can forgive even someone who is dead. Forgiveness allows us to release someone who has harmed us in some way. We release the right to have the person 'get what they deserve.'

"Forgiveness is a gift to us. It isn't something we do for the offender. It is something God does for us. Forgiveness, apart from the love of God, is impossible."

I know I've forgiven Vanessa, Jenny thought. *Why am I so suspicious of her?*

"Just because you forgive someone," the pastor continued, "doesn't automatically mean *restoration* of the relationship. If someone has abused you, for example, you can forgive the person without reentering that relationship. In fact, returning to an abusive relationship is probably not wise."

Restoration. That's the word Colton used about Vanessa and Daniel.

"Restoration occurs when the person who caused the harm acknowledges the harm and asks for and receives forgiveness. In legal terms, restoration requires restitution or repayment. As Christians, we know that our Lord has already made restitution. We can forgive anyone anything because Jesus has already paid the debt—not just our debt, but theirs also.

"How can *we* hold a debt when our Lord has already forgiven it?

"I love the fact that both *rest*oration and *rest*itution begin with *rest*. Rest in Him. He is able. He is the great Healer and Restorer of our souls."

The choir stood as the congregation took a collective breath and leaned back against the pews.

Restoration. It echoed in Jenny's heart.

"You are my sunshine, my only sunshine," Jenny sang to Sunny as she brushed. Glory sneaked around Sunny's hindquarters to bump Jenny playfully with her head. The filly's head now came up to Jenny's shoulders. "You little imp," Jenny chastised, rubbing the filly's back. Glory loved a good back scratch, and she positioned herself under Jenny's fingers. Her little lip twitched with delight. Jenny grinned.

"Pretty irresistible," Daniel commented from the stall door.

Jenny glanced up at his voice. "Yup," she sighed. "Both of them are . . . well, let's just say I can't imagine life without them."

"I know what you mean," he replied quietly. "I can't imagine life without Fury. And I thank *you* for that."

"You should thank *Him* for that," Jenny responded. "It really was His idea. I knew it was true after He said it."

"I thank you both," Daniel said softly. "And I thank you for insisting that Aunt Vanessa come here."

"Really?" Jenny questioned. "I . . . I don't know, it seems so sudden, she and Colton. I can't help but wonder . . ."

"What? What do you wonder?" Daniel asked.

"I don't know. She's so different. I can't help it. I just feel like she may be up to something."

"Like what?"

"Like . . . I don't know. I'm afraid she's brainwashed him or something."

"Why, Jennifer Lynne! I do believe you are jealous!" Daniel chortled.

"Jealous? Of whom?" she snorted.

"Colton has been your good friend, your teacher. Now he's in love. He hasn't had any time for you."

"That's not true!" she huffed. "I'm just . . . concerned for him."

"Well, he seems happy to me," Daniel replied. "And I'm pretty sure that, at the age of 43, he's able to take care of himself."

"Daniel." Jenny glanced around to be certain they were alone. "What if she's conning him? To . . . I don't know . . . get his money or horses?"

"Jenny," Daniel responded, "do you remember what you told me when I was so shocked to hear about your mom's pregnancy?"

"No," she answered.

"You told me I'd better get used to a new life. Jen, Vanessa is a new Life. She has accepted Christ. She is a new creation. Get used to it."

He turned on his heel and marched toward the hay barn. Jenny's thoughts swirled for a moment.

I was going to witness to her. I had it all planned. I'm the one who started with her. I had to beg Daniel to let her come here. Lord! You said I would be the one to heal their hearts! Not Colton.

No, my lovely child. I am the one who heals hearts. I told you that healing would come through you, not from you. And it did. You allowed Me to express My Love to Vanessa. Your forgiveness touched her in a way nobody else could have.

And then Jenny's spirit knew Truth. *Lord,* her heart cried, *I'm such a jerk!*

No, you are Mine. You are who you are because of whose you are. And you are Mine. Just keep your eyes on Me, not Vanessa or Colton. They are Mine too.

Jenny bowed her head and put her arms around Sunny's neck. The mare blew warm breath on Jenny's back.

Think of Me, hugging you.

Jenny stayed right there.

Chapter Fifteen

Vanessa found Jenny still standing with Sunny.

"Hey, Jen," she sang cheerfully from the electric wheelchair.

"Hello, Vanessa," Jenny replied.

"Can we talk, and go for a walk?"

"Sure," Jenny answered.

"Let's go to the pond," Vanessa suggested. "It's my private thinking spot."

"How come I never found this?" Jenny asked herself aloud, looking at the still, serene water. Lily pads and wooden decoys floated on the surface. A frog squeaked and splashed into the water as they passed.

Vanessa guided the electric wheelchair along a path around the edge, right to a picnic table. She managed, with Jenny's help, to transfer herself from the chair to the table's bench.

"Oof. It's getting easier . . . I think," she said with a grimace.

What does she want to talk about? Jenny wondered, sitting on her hands.

"I need to ask your forgiveness, Jenny," Vanessa said softly. "My problem is that I don't know where to begin. I was so angry, and I've done so many things to hurt you and Sunny."

"What has changed?" Jenny asked.

"I have. And I haven't just changed. I now understand why nothing in my life worked before. You were right, Jenny. It's got nothing to do with religion. I'm so glad you said that to me. Colton introduced me to Jesus, right here, in this very spot. He explained that Jesus could transform me, not just change me. It's been amazing."

"I'm so glad," Jenny whispered sincerely.

"The pastor today made me realize that I haven't asked you to forgive me. I want restoration. I want to be your friend."

That word. Again!

"So, Jenny, will you forgive me . . . for everything? I've hated you and Sunny; I've tried everything in my power to take her from you. I hated the fact that you had the relationship with her that I lost with Honey. I hated the fact that you *could* take her from me . . . It made me feel just the way I did after my dad sold Honey. I felt powerless and hurt.

"That night when you two broke the world record, I wanted to die. There you were, on *my* horse, the horse I couldn't control, doing what I should have been doing . . . and you had the audacity to forgive me . . . in public, in front of the whole world.

"My world was so immersed in hatred and a need to control, that it controlled me. And it almost destroyed me and everything I now care about.

"You know, right after I got here, the *first* Sunday morning, Colton says over breakfast, 'We're leavin' for church in forty minutes. Daniel will help you to the truck when you're ready.'" Vanessa shook her head as she remembered. "I was so mad! Church! The very last place I wanted to go was church. I had barely brushed my hair in three weeks. Dan pushed me back to my cabin and helped me as much as he could. I was being very mean. After I called him a couple names he left, just left me there to get ready by myself. And you know what? I couldn't even lift the hairbrush. So there I am, helpless, grungy, feeling about as low and disgusting as I've ever felt. Colton breezes into my cabin, swoops me into his arms. Patrick pushed my wheelchair and then tossed it in the truck, and I'm going to church."

"And how was your first church service?" Jenny asked, chuckling and shaking her head. "I can just see Colton doing that."

Vanessa looked down at her hands for a moment. When she looked up, her eyes were shiny with tears. "It was amazing, Jen. Those women there, they took me in, like an orphan. They had a reception . . . for me. To welcome me. *Me!* They made me feel loved. For the first time in a very long time, I felt loved. The only other time I remember feeling that was when you had your arms around me in my car, keeping me alive."

"Really?" Jenny asked.

"Really. I am grateful for the accident, Jen. I happily give up my leg, to gain . . . this. This peace, this freedom. This love. Colton's and God's. I have never experienced anything like it in my life. I have you and Sunny to thank. You told me you could help me find Life. I had no idea what you meant. So, can you forgive me for everything I've done or wanted to do?"

"Yes, Vanessa. Can you forgive me for being so suspicious?"

"Absolutely."

"One more thing," Vanessa said. "Can we go see Sunny? I'd love to see if she can forgive me."

Jenny held her breath as they approached the barn. Sunny heard the wheelchair and poked her head out to investigate the noise.

"Hey, Sunny girl," Jenny announced softly, "this is my new friend, Vanessa DuBois, soon to be Vanessa Wright."

Vanessa started giggling.

"What?" asked Jenny. "What is so funny?"

"My name will be Vanessa Wright. I've never *been* right until now, and now I'll be Wright. It's just so funny!"

"Well, Sunny seems to approve of Vanessa Wright," said Jenny.

Sunny gently sniffed Vanessa's hands and then her face. Vanessa slowly raised her right hand to stroke Sunny's neck. Sunny sighed and relaxed, her eyes soft.

"That means more to me than almost anything," Vanessa choked tearfully. "I feel like I can explain things to you . . . sort of. Sunny doesn't understand, and she still forgives me. Incredible!"

Restoration.

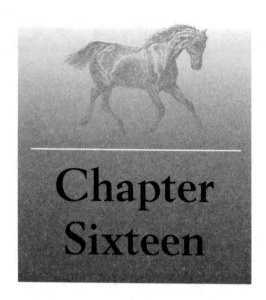

Chapter Sixteen

"Therapeutic Riding." It was right there in the phone book under "T." Jenny dialed the number.

"New Life Therapy Center, director speaking," a voice said.

Jenny grinned at the name. "We'd like to visit your center if possible," she said, and told the director what they hoped to do.

"We'd love to show you our facility. When can you come?"

"Would this afternoon work?" Jenny asked hopefully.

"How 'bout two?"

"Perfect. See you then."

Jenny conned Daniel into driving her to the center. The director showed them a horse-mounting platform, some mounting techniques, and exercises for amputees.

Jenny and Daniel drove back to Cedar Creek armed with advice and building plans. Daniel and Patrick gathered some tools and began to work immediately. After two hours, they had built a platform.

An hour after that, they drove Vanessa to the therapeutic center. For several hours, she learned safety rules and exercises to strengthen her left leg, her stump, and her upper body.

The next day the four of them tried to re-create the therapy at home with Honey. Daniel helped Vanessa onto the platform; Jenny held Honey; and Patrick stayed on the opposite side of Honey to ensure Vanessa didn't slide off headfirst while mounting.

Honey seemed to understand what was happening. The old mare didn't even stamp at the flies landing on her legs. Jenny nudged the insects away with the tip of her boot.

"I can't wait for the first frost to kill all these blood-sucking horseflies," she announced to no one in particular.

"Amen," agreed Patrick.

"Oof," Vanessa complained, looking up from her belly as she draped herself over the saddle. "Now what do I do?" she asked. "This isn't a particularly ladylike pose."

"Now you're supposed to use your arms to raise your body and throw your right leg over the saddle," Jenny said, pantomiming as she tried to recall the correct move.

Honey's ears pricked up with interest, watching Jenny.

"That might work if your arms weren't toothpicks," Vanessa groaned.

"Come on, Aunt V," Daniel encouraged. "You can do it."

"I'm slipping," Vanessa wailed.

"I gotcha, V," Jenny assured her, grabbing Vanessa's leg and holding it gently.

"One, two, three," Vanessa said and gave a mighty push, throwing her stump over the back of the saddle. She was up!

"Well done," Jenny said, smiling up at her.

Vanessa's eyes sparkled. "I can take it from here," she informed them. She picked up the reins and clucked to Honey. The mare began walking. Two clucks and she trotted. Vanessa said, "Walk, Honey," in a low voice, and the mare slowed to a walk. As Vanessa guided the old mare back to the platform, tears welled in her eyes. "She remembers," she whispered in awe. "I voice-trained her . . . twenty years ago, and she still remembers."

Restoration.

As Jenny watched Vanessa and Honey together, her heart sang. *Thank you, Lord,* she prayed. Vanessa was now cantering comfortably, her face shining with joy as she rode.

That's how I feel when I watch you and Sunny too.
You make my heart sing.

Tomorrow. We go home tomorrow, Jenny thought. For some reasons she couldn't wait to get home to Sonrise Farm Too; for other reasons she could have happily stayed at Cedar Creek forever. The place had a peace and tranquility about it that beckoned her heart.

Like heaven?

She slipped out into the early morning mist. The trees were just starting to change color. Jenny felt a sudden impulse to visit the spot where Sunny had escaped the previous year. *Almost exactly a year ago,* she thought.

Glory.

What do you mean? her heart wondered.

Glory means "My love revealed."

Christ in me, the hope of glory. Is that what it means?

Christ in you, expressing love and Life to others.
That is what you were born to do. That is Life. That is
freedom. It is irresistible.

Her heart knew it was true.

A little later, Jenny and Sunny walked through the woods in the morning light. Glory followed, sometimes close, sometimes lagging behind to investigate something. When the filly got too far behind she would gallop to catch up, squealing her baby squeal.

Sunny felt sound and strong under the saddle. "Shall we trot?" Jenny suggested. She sat up, looked ahead, and just thought about going faster. *Lovely, floaty trot.*

"We'll have to let Dr. Davis check you out, Sunny," Jenny said, laughing. "I think you are fine."

The big copper bell at Cedar Creek rang out. "Uh-oh. Better get back." Jenny turned her head and then her waist to see if she could direct Sunny to turn around without the reins. She had just begun to lift the left rein when Sunny did a neat pirouette and headed back.

"Look at you!" Daniel crowed as Jenny returned to the barn. "First ride?"

"Yup, and she was great." Jenny smiled. "She rolled yesterday for the first time. I knew she was OK after that."

"Colton is going to miss you around here," Daniel said.

"I'm going to miss you too," she said, nodding.

"You won't miss me as much as you think," he said, winking mysteriously. "Come and eat before it gets cold. I made pancakes."

At breakfast, Vanessa was so excited she could hardly speak. "OK, OK. Here's my idea," she said. Her pancakes sat cold and wilting on the plate in front of her. "I talked to the director at the New Life Therapy Center. He's very interested in opening another center, somewhere else—like in Virginia!"

"Yeah, so?" Jenny said, stuffing pancakes in her mouth at the same time.

"So, I've got this farm," Vanessa continued, "just sitting there. Full of unhappy memories for *me*. The center can use it to help people. To help people *heal.*"

Restoration. Glory.

After breakfast, Daniel helped Jenny pack her tack trunk.

"So you and Patrick are going to be directors of a therapeutic riding place?" Jenny asked.

"No, we'll hire an actual director. Someone who knows something about . . . directing," Daniel explained. "Patrick and I will be the overseers and do our own thing at the farm."

"And what thing would *that* be?" Jenny inquired with curiosity.

"We're going to rescue and rehabilitate horses. Some of them will go to the riding program, some will be placed with more advanced riders. We'll do our best to place as many horses as we can. The farm is perfect. It has the quarantine barn for horses from auctions and all those little paddocks for horses that just need some time and groceries."

"So, that farm, the farm where Sunny and Fury were abused, will now become a rescue and rehab for horses *and* people." Jenny could only shake her head with wonder.

Lord, you are so funny, turning Vanessa's farm into a haven.

Restoration, He whispered to her heart.

What else will you restore? she asked.

You'll see, He answered.

Chapter Seventeen

"They stole my idea," Kathy complained as she and Jenny trotted side by side. Magnum reached sideways, trying to nuzzle Sunny's nose. Sunny pinned back her ears and gave him a quick nip. Magnum tossed his head with surprise.

Jenny rubbed Sunny's neck. "Your baby is fine at the barn. No need to take it out on Magnum."

" 'Cedar Creek Too.' Couldn't they come up with their own clever name for the therapy center?"

"You know what they say," Jenny said, rubbing Sunny's neck. "Imitation is the highest form of flattery. It'll be fun having Daniel and Patrick so close by."

"How are the wedding plans going?" Kathy inquired. "Talked to V lately?"

"I guess they're fine. I haven't talked to Vanessa or Dan. Maybe I'll call tonight and check on them. We're almost in the home stretch. Two weeks to go!"

Jenny tried calling Daniel in the late afternoon. Patrick answered the phone. "Hello, Cedar Creek Too, may I help you?"

"Hey, Patrick," Jenny greeted. "Dan there?"

"Nope," was the reply.

"When do you expect him?"

"Don't know."

"Patrick, what is going on?" Jenny demanded, feeling annoyed.

"Can't say," he replied, and Jenny could *hear* the smile in his voice.

"Can you ask him to call me?" Jenny begged, putting on her best sickly sweet tone.

"I'll sure try," he promised.

"OK, Mysterio. See ya."

"Bye."

That was rude, she thought.

Daniel called Jenny just before dinner, on his cell phone. The static was terrible.

"Dan, where are you? You sound like you're in a helicopter."

"Sorry, Jen. Your guess is close, though. I'm in a bus station. In California."

"California!" Jenny gasped. "What are you doing there?"

"Looking for my grandfather."

"What? Why?"

"To invite him to Aunt V's wedding. She really wants him there."

"I thought he was, you know, not so nice."

"He's not," Daniel conceded. "But he's the only dad she has here on earth, and if I can find him I'll try to get him there."

"Does Vanessa know what you're doing?" Jenny questioned.

"No. This was Colton's brainstorm. We don't want her to be disappointed. It's been a couple years since anyone has heard from him."

"Have you seen *your* dad?" Jenny asked.

"Staying with him actually."

"You are kidding! How's it going?"

"It's all right," he affirmed. "Dad looks older, and he seems tired. He's not sure what to make of me either. The new me. Anyway, I'm on Grandpa's trail. I talked to a guy yesterday who sees Gramps from time to time."

"Well, good luck, Daniel," Jenny said.

"Luck! You don't believe in luck, and neither do I," he chided gently. "I'm here because He sent me. Finding Grandpa is His problem, plus God is probably the *only* one who knows where Grandpa is. Don't wish me luck. Pray for me."

"I will," Jenny chuckled.

And he was gone.

Jenny smiled, pondering the change in him. He had accepted Jesus the previous year in Colton's greatroom. She had prayed with him after watching the video of Fury with Colton. This was the first open declaration of God's leading she'd heard Daniel make. He had made comments before, in passing. But this was different. This was bold.

What you are up to, Lord?

Restoration.

Jenny didn't get a chance to call Cedar Creek before she sat down to eat. After dinner, as she cleared the plates, the phone rang. It was Vanessa.

"Can I talk to your mom, Jen?" Vanessa asked cheerfully.

"Uh . . . sure. Let me get her," Jenny responded, feeling a little confused. "Don't you want to talk to me?" she asked.

"I *will* talk to you, but I need to ask your mom an important question," Vanessa responded.

Jenny lowered the phone. "Mom!" she bellowed. "Phone for you."

"How's it going there?" Jenny asked Vanessa as she waited for her mother to pick up the extension.

"It's going," Vanessa replied. "I just wish I had more time."

"Why don't you postpone?" Jenny suggested.

"No. I'd rather marry Colton in a feed sack than postpone."

"That'd be funny," Jenny said, imagining a feed-sack dress. "You'd have horses following you down the aisle."

"I may have horses following me down the aisle anyway," Vanessa quipped.

"Hello, this is Judy Thomas," Jenny's mother broke in.

"I'll talk to you later, Vanessa," Jenny said, hanging up.

"That's a promise," returned Vanessa.

Jenny went back to clearing the table and rinsing dishes. The water running over her hands was warm and comfortable. It made a slight swishing sound as it came from the spigot. *Shtoration. Reshtoration. Restoration.* **Restoration**.

She grinned as she finished her dinner chore. "Lord," she said. "You are so amazing. Talking to me about Vanessa through the water pipes."

And then it was Jenny's turn to talk to Vanessa.

"Here's the deal," Vanessa started. "Your mom says it's all right for you to come up with Kathy tomorrow and help me."

"Help you with what?" Jenny asked.

"Help me practice going down the aisle. I want to surprise Colton by walking down the aisle without a cane or crutch. I'm almost there, but I need more time. With Dan gone, I just can't practice enough. My physical therapist says I'm doing fine and shouldn't push it . . . and Colton pays her. So she doesn't listen to me. Will you help?"

Jenny smiled as she heard some of the old Vanessa peeking out from the new-creation Vanessa.

"Sure, I'd love to help. Any way I can. You sure are tenacious, V."

"Like a bulldog," Vanessa agreed. "Call Kathy then," she instructed. "I just talked to her, and you two can work out the details between you. I'll see you tomorrow."

"Tomorrow it is."

Jenny hung up the phone.

"Take your algebra books with you," Mrs. Thomas called from downstairs as Jenny headed to her room to pack.

"Yes, Mom," she muttered, pulling them out from under the bed. "I was hoping you guys could stay here and get some rest," she said to the thick textbooks. *A couple pair of jeans, some boots, and I'm done.*

When Kathy arrived, she and Jenny hooked up the big four-horse gooseneck trailer to Kathy's truck. Magnum walked into the front section, and Kathy closed the partition. Sunny and Glory walked into the second half.

"That filly is gorgeous, Jen," Kathy breathed as Jenny closed the trailer door. "You see her every day, so the changes aren't as obvious to you. When I see her, she takes my breath away."

"Thanks, Kathy," Jenny said, glowing. "I just love her."

"Let's do some trail riding at Colton's," Kathy suggested. "Maybe Vanessa could go with us on Honey."

"That'd be good," Jenny replied, pulling the passenger door shut and buckling her seatbelt. "I have a feeling the future Mrs. Wright has her own plans for us. She's pretty focused on one thing. We'll see if she lets us go anywhere."

Chapter Eighteen

As Jenny opened the trailer to fetch Sunny and Glory, Colton burst through the back door.

"Jen! Kathy! What are you doing here? The wedding's not for two weeks!"

"Uh . . . we're here to help Vanessa with the finishing touches," Kathy said quickly.

"That's right!" Jenny agreed. "And I'm the maid of honor. I *need* to be here."

"Well, that's great," Colton said with a grin. "Daniel's cottage is empty and clean if you want to take it. It's next door to Vanessa's. Come on in for some lunch when you're ready." He rubbed Glory's neck as he passed by. "She is lovely, Jen," he murmured, stepping back to get a better look. The filly followed him as he backed up. "And she's as sweet as her mama," he said, smiling, and he stroked Glory's face.

"Thank you," Jenny said and smiled back. "She's my girl!"

"See you inside," Colton said warmly. "I'm really glad you're here." He sauntered back to the main house.

Jenny spied Vanessa waving from the kitchen, and she waved back. "Let's get these guys situated. I'll put the girls in the paddock out back. Is that where you want Magnum?"

"Sure. I'll check the water trough and unload the feed."

Lunch was leftover cold pizza.

"You eat it like this?" Jenny asked Colton doubtfully, poking at the plasticlike, congealed cheese. "Do you mind if I microwave it?"

"Heavens, no! Go right ahead." Colton laughed, taking a big bite of his slice.

"Would you zap mine too, please?" Kathy asked, handing her paper plate to Jenny.

"Is this an example of the food we will get at the wedding?" Jenny asked.

"No. We've ordered *fresh* pizza for the wedding!" Colton chortled.

"My physical therapist is coming just after lunch," Vanessa whispered. "I want you to watch her so you can help me later."

"Done," Jenny agreed.

The frazzled female therapist arrived two minutes later in a white van. Jenny and Kathy helped Vanessa to the huge family room, which had been transformed into a physical therapy center.

"OK, Ms. DuBois," the therapist huffed. "I want you to use the handrails if you need to. Let's try to get at least ten steps today."

Balance, Jenny thought. *That's the problem. She can't keep her balance.* She watched Vanessa totter painfully. *She's staring at the floor.*

Vanessa grabbed the support bar and stared at Jenny. "Do you see what I mean?" she demanded.

Jenny nodded. "I do see what you mean!"

Vanessa looked intently into Jenny's eyes. "What are you saying? Should I do something different?"

Jenny glanced at the therapist. "I don't want to butt in . . ."

The physical therapist threw up her hands. "I quit!" she shrieked and stormed out, slamming the door behind her.

"My, my!" Kathy exclaimed. "*She's* just a little angry."

"She's my third therapist," Vanessa said sheepishly. "I must be difficult to work with or something."

"Or *something*," Kathy quipped.

Jenny glanced at Kathy. *What have we gotten ourselves into?* she thought to herself. "Let's start with the horse," Jenny suggested. "I'll tack Honey up, and we'll work in the round pen."

"I don't want to *ride,* Jenny. I want to walk!" Vanessa insisted.

"This is necessary for you to walk," Jenny said, smiling. "Haven't you heard the phrase 'you gotta ride before you can walk'?"

"I believe that's an old cowboy motto," Kathy added with a grin.

Vanessa stared at Jenny for a few moments. "OK," she agreed. "Nothing else has worked. I'm desperate."

"First of all, Vanessa," Jenny began, "you have to keep your eyes up and focused on where you want to wind up. Don't stare at the ground unless that's where you want to go. Try this now, on your own . . . foot." *Almost said "own two feet,"* she realized with a little fear. "Try looking back to your left, and down. Now try to lift your left foot."

"I can't!" Vanessa cried.

"Exactly. Now, look back, left, and up. Now lift your left foot."

Vanessa lifted her left foot with a perplexed look. "What is going on?"

"Nothing much," Jenny explained. "Your body has natural weight shifts. They are almost unnoticeable to us. They are incredibly noticeable to our horses. Honey will be your best teacher. We need to get you shifting your weight so you can move your feet, uh, foot, feet . . . I'm sorry, Vanessa. What do you want me to say? Feet or foot?"

"You can say feet. I have two; one just happens to be plastic or rubber or something. Left and right are fine. I *do* know my left and right," Vanessa said pointedly.

"I can see why you've gone through a couple PTs," Jenny replied. "Are you always this cooperative?"

"I'm sorry," Vanessa sighed. "I really want to walk. I'm feeling desperate, and it makes me angry."

"Well, getting mad at your helpers will just make them leave," Jenny said, smiling.

"I know, I know. What can I do? This anger just rages up inside me. I guess I'm like my dad. I've been angry for so long, I don't even know where it comes from," Vanessa cried.

"You know what, Vanessa?" Kathy interjected. "As a believer you have a new identity. You can choose to believe what God says about you, or you can continue to believe what you say about you."

"What do you mean?" Vanessa questioned.

"I mean, you are no longer Vanessa, the angry, rich divorcee, horse owner . . . and on and on. You are now Vanessa, the bride of Christ. Righteous and holy. You can see yourself as that old thing or the new creation. Once you see yourself as the new creation, you are less likely to behave like that old thing."

"Well, that's very easy to say," Vanessa sniffed.

Remind her that she is Mine.

"Vanessa," Jenny blurted. "It's really a question of ownership. Who do you belong to?"

"Why, to myself," she huffed, drawing herself up.

"No-o-o," Jenny said. "You belong to Him. Not in a slave-like way, against your will. In a 'reunion with Honey' way. In a 'He loves you and He is able' way."

"I don't get it," Vanessa murmured softly. "I want to, but I don't."

"It seems to me that you are so focused on walking down the aisle by yourself—that you are by yourself once again. You are determined to do something apart from Him."

"Why doesn't He want me to walk?" Vanessa asked, pouting. "I want it more than anything!"

"Bingo," announced Kathy. "You want it more than *any-thing*. Walking is not Life, Vanessa. He is Life. And He is faithful and true. Any life we struggle to find apart from Him is worthless. Stop focusing your heart on walking. Focus your heart on Him. He is your heart's home. Everything else will fall into place once you recognize you are home."

"I still don't get what He has to do with walking!" Vanessa said sharply. "You talk about Him like He's right here. Well, I don't *feel* Him right here. So what has that got to do with walking?"

I'll show her the video of Fury, the one Daniel loved to watch, Jenny thought.

"Time out," Jenny called. "Let's make some popcorn and watch something special."

"Jen. Have you been listening to me?" Vanessa asked loudly. Jenny looked into the ice-blue eyes and saw flowing tears. "I *must* walk. For Colton. I don't want him to marry a cripple."

"Whoa, I heard that." Colton's deep voice came from the doorway. "Vanessa, you are no cripple. You *were* a cripple before you came to Christ. You are whole, a new creation. If any man or woman is in Christ, he or she is a new creature; the old things have passed away; behold, new things have come."

Vanessa stared at him like a frightened deer. Then her eyes dropped and her shoulders began shaking as she wept silently.

Colton took her into his arms and held her until the shaking stopped.

"All my life," she choked, "I've been a disappointment. To my father, my husband, myself. I just don't know how to stop trying." She looked up at Colton with such sadness that Jenny had to look away. "I would want to die if I disappointed you."

"Oh, Vanessa," he breathed. "You can't disappoint me. It's not possible. You are in Christ. That is all I could ask for."

"Really?" she whispered. "That's all?"

"Really," he confirmed. "I'll carry you down the aisle if I need to."

One corner of Vanessa's mouth twitched and then curved up. She rubbed her nose with the back of her hand. "Anyone have a tissue?" she asked. "OK, Miss Thomas. Let's get to work. With Honey."

"Yes, ma'am," Jenny said and saluted.

We can watch the ride later, Jenny thought.

"Eyes first, Vanessa, then your belly button. Focus your eyes on where you want to go, then point your belly where you want to go. Then push with your opposite leg, and use the rein if she hasn't turned. After a couple times, she'll figure it out."

"It's so weird, Jen!" Vanessa exclaimed as the mare began turning in response to Vanessa's eyes. "It's like she's reading my mind!"

"Nope, no mind reading going on here," Jenny said, smiling. "It's the way your body shifts weight. When your head is up and your focus is straight, you sit evenly. When you turn your head, you change the way you sit. Your horse feels that, and if you'll give her the chance to respond, you won't even need the reins. I'll show you what I mean. Stay here." Jenny sprinted into the barn. Glory, sleeping soundly, startled at the sound of Jenny's approaching footsteps. The filly snorted indignantly as she rose.

"Hey, girls," Jenny greeted the drowsy horses. "Let's go play." She pulled the rope halter onto Sunny's nose and led her toward the round pen where Vanessa and Honey waited. Glory followed close behind, bumping Sunny playfully with her nose. Sunny pinned her ears and lifted a hind foot in warning. Glory tossed her head and took off bucking.

Jenny couldn't help grinning. She was still grinning as she and Sunny walked through the gate to the round pen. She closed the gate and then climbed on the third rung in order to clamber onto Sunny's back.

"Oof, not very graceful," she grunted. "OK, Vanessa," she called as she settled herself, "I am going to start with eyes." Jenny focused on a spot straight across the round pen. "Now, I'll turn my eyes left, then my belly button." She didn't need to go further, since Sunny turned almost immediately. "Now, I put some energy in my body and . . . we're trotting. Now, I deflate," and Jenny breathed out and slumped over. Sunny stopped.

"That's amazing!" Vanessa cried.

"That's what you need to do when you walk," Jenny said. "You need to make your weight shift help you. When you stare at the ground, you can't move. Here. Let's put your saddle on Sunny and *you* ride her. She'll tell us if you're doing it right."

"But what if—" Vanessa started.

"What if what?" Jenny asked. "She'll be fine. You are *not*

the same person who harmed her, and she *has* forgiven you."

Jenny gave Vanessa a leg up. "Who-o-e-e-e," Vanessa breathed. "I had forgotten how tall she is. It's a long way down." She rubbed Sunny's neck. "It's amazing to be back on her. You know something? This is the first time Sunny has ever stood still with me on her. She used to go crazy. It took three grooms holding her for me to mount."

"Well, that was the old you. That person is gone. Remember what Colton said? Behold, the new has come!"

"So how does this work?" Vanessa asked as she and Sunny began walking around the pen.

"Start with your eyes. That's all you'll need with her."

And that was all it took. Sunny turned sharply almost at the same time as Vanessa focused. The mare then turned sharply again as Vanessa's eyes found Jenny's. "Incredible," she murmured.

By the end of the hour, Vanessa and Sunny were trotting and cantering smoothly without reins.

"Now you are ready to walk," Jenny announced. "Let's give it a try."

"What is wrong with me?" Vanessa wailed. "It's been a week, and I still can't walk more than two feet. My wedding is in a week, and I . . . I can't stand it."

"Well," Kathy sighed. "You're doing what you need to do. You just need more practice. It's simply a matter of time."

"I don't have time," Vanessa huffed. "I'm out of time."

Kathy didn't answer.

What should we do, Lord? Jenny asked.

Show her the video of Fury. The movie Daniel loved.

"Vanessa," Jenny announced. "Come with me. I want to show you something."

In the family room of the main house, Jenny, Kathy, and Vanessa sat down in front of the TV and VCR. *Déjà vu,* Jenny thought, sitting next to Vanessa and eating popcorn by the fistful. *A year ago I sat here doing exactly the same thing with Daniel. Lord, You knew this would happen! You were preparing me and Vanessa for this moment a year ago.*

Yes.

Kathy hit the Play button on the remote control, and Jenny held her breath.

"Huh!" Vanessa gasped as a thin, terrified Fury appeared on the screen. "Why, oh why are you showing me this?"

"Just watch. It'll be all right," Jenny assured her. "Here you see Fury running in the round pen, and Colton outside the pen, reading. Fury stops running, so Colton picks up the bucket, inches a little closer, and continues reading."

"Why is he doing that?" Vanessa asked. "Why not just go in?"

"Well, Fury's opinion of human beings was . . . not so nice. Sort of like some folks' opinion of God. We form our beliefs on previous experience, and so do horses. Colton was making sure he didn't put too much emotional pressure on him. This is about fellowship and harmony. We want horses to want to be with us."

"How do you do that?"

"By knowing a little about how horses think and what they want," Jenny explained. "See, horses and people want comfort. We both want a sense of 'OK'-ness. It's what I call Life. Jesus came to this earth so we could have Life. Anything apart from Him is death. The round pen represents time, or our lifespan. See, Colton is not bound by the pen, and God is not bound in time. Time is just a tool He uses to reveal Himself to us. Fury is doing everything he knows to find life. He believes he is trapped with a predator. So he does all the horse things he knows to do—running, bucking, looking outside the pen for help. And Colton just waits. It's the same as the way Jesus waits for us while we try all the tricks we think will bring us Life."

Jenny glanced at Vanessa.

"Go on!" Vanessa urged, spellbound.

"And here, Fury decides to give up on his way of doing business. Fury *chooses* to trust Colton. Not because he feels like it, but because he sees the futility of life his way. Surrender brings peace, comfort, Life. Fury takes a step of faith and finds comfort with Colton as his leader. The other neat picture here is that they are both in the pen, like Jesus and you in your life. It doesn't matter what you do or where you go, He is with you. Because He's in you.

"Your attempts to get what you want apart from Him only bring you pain. Not because He wants to hurt you, of course. They hurt because you were never designed to meet your own needs. That is His deal. Honey is your deal, right? She never worries about tomorrow, if you will feed her, why Sunny gets more food than she does. She just loves you and trusts you and does whatever you ask her to do."

"But what about Fury?" Vanessa asked with a stricken look. "I didn't look after him. I starved him. How do you know God won't do that to me? It only seems fair after all I've done. How do you know He's not punishing me by keeping me from walking?"

"I can know that God won't do that to you because He says He won't. And Vanessa, think about it. Jesus loves you so much, He would rather die than live without you. He created you to live in Him. Anything apart from that brings emptiness. Anything apart from that isn't Life. You are where you are supposed to be. He was thinking about His moment with you last year when Dan and I sat here, having a similar conversation. Vanessa, He has loved you, followed you, protected you, and waited for you to choose Him. Let *Him* decide whether you will walk down the aisle. Then you are free to give it your best shot without having the pressure of 'making it happen.' "

Vanessa melted into a mass of tears. "I hear what you are saying, and I *think* I understand. I can trust Him to take care of all the things I've tried to take care of myself. All the things that drive me."

"Yes," Jenny said, nodding. "*That* is freedom, Vanessa. Our only job is to keep our eyes on Him. When we do that, everything else is simple."

"Hey! Is that my favorite video?" Daniel asked from the doorway.

"Dan! What are you doing here?" Jenny shrieked, leaping up to hug him.

"I have a surprise for Vanessa," he said with a big grin.

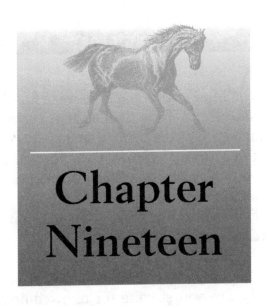

Chapter Nineteen

"Daddy?" Vanessa questioned, staring at the haggard, gray-haired man standing before her. She rose and walked slowly toward him, looking intently into his face. The man didn't look up but stood hunched and uncomfortable, crushing his crumpled hat in his hands.

She approached him warily, like a dog that has been kicked a time or two. The man lifted his eyes as she stopped directly in front of him. Jenny saw hopeless, pathetic eyes. His chin quivered as he spoke. "Vanessa?" he whispered.

"Oh, Daddy!" she cried, throwing her arms around his neck. He stood rock still, hat in one hand, the other hand hanging at his side. Slowly, like a statue coming to life, he raised his arms and tightened them around her until he hugged her close. "Vanessa," he wept. "I thought I'd never see you again. I . . . I'm sorry. So sorry."

Vanessa looked at his face, nodded, and then threw her arms around his neck again.

Jenny caught Daniel's glance. He smiled, his eyes overflowing with joy.

"Jenny, Kathy, Colton," Vanessa announced shakily. "This is my dad, Kevin Perkins."

Colton shook Mr. Perkins' hand. "Nice to finally meet you, sir," he said sincerely. "We're thrilled that you're here."

Jenny walked across the room to shake Mr. Perkins' hand. *He's shorter than I thought he'd be,* she thought.

"Vanessa, do you realize you just walked across the room?" Jenny whispered.

Vanessa clapped her hand over her mouth in shock. ***Restoration.***

"So, Daddy, are you staying for my wedding?" Vanessa asked at the kitchen table after everyone settled down.

"That's why I'm here," Mr. Perkins replied.

"What about getting married on horseback?" Colton asked. Then he said as an aside, "Jen, pass me the ketchup, please."

"What?" Vanessa squawked.

"You know, the wedding on horseback," he repeated.

Vanessa stared at him, speechless. "I . . . I . . . I love it! But I've already bought my dress, and it's not a dress I can ride in."

"So? We'll get you a new dress. If you want to."

"Man alive, it sure is exciting around here!" Vanessa teased, fanning herself.

"Never dull," Jenny said, grinning.

"Daddy," Vanessa said, suddenly serious. "I want you to come to the barn and meet someone. Someone you haven't seen for a long time."

"Do you want company?" Colton inquired.

"No, I'm all right," Vanessa assured him. "We won't be long."

She hopped on her electric scooter. Colton watched the two as they meandered slowly toward the barn.

"So, Daniel. You are the hero of the day. How did you find him?"

"I just started hanging out in the parks in LA," Daniel said with a shrug. "I had a picture of him and asked everyone I saw if they'd ever seen him. He was living in a homeless shelter. After I found him, I took him to my folks' house for a week. It took three days to convince him to come back East with me. He was sure Vanessa hated him."

"What do you think he'll do now?" Colton asked.

"I've no idea," Daniel replied. "I'm not sure he knows."

"Well, good for you for finding him. I know Vanessa is grateful."

"I hope she still feels that way in a week."

"It'll be fine," Colton said, patting Daniel's back.

"This one is beautiful," Jenny cooed, pointing to a dress in the catalog.

"Too frilly," Vanessa sniffed.

"This one is nice, V," suggested Kathy, poring over a different catalog.

"That one *is* nice!" Vanessa agreed, looking up from her magazine. "What's the turn-around time?"

"You can express-mail it. It'll be here in three days."

"Do it! I need a size six."

"What did your dad say when he saw Honey?" Jenny asked.

"He started crying again, which made me start crying. He couldn't believe it. You know, *I* still can't believe it. All the pain and hurt in my life. It's like God is going through and taking care of each burden. It's amazing!"

Sitting up straight, Vanessa thought for a moment.

"Now we need to figure out where the seats and tables will be, since we'll be on horseback. And we should probably practice," she mused. "I guess Colton will ride Polo."

"Probably," Jenny agreed. *Maybe. Maybe not.* She got up and wandered away to find Colton.

Jenny found him behind the house. Putting her finger to her lips, she whispered something in Colton's ear.

"I think it's a wonderful idea," Colton whispered back. "We'll have matching palominos at the altar. Make a great photo op. So it's settled. Vanessa will be on Honey; I'll be on Sunny. Oh-h-h!" he groaned. "They even rhyme."

Vanessa's dress arrived on Tuesday. It fit perfectly, as though it was made just for her. She spun around in front of the full-length mirror. "That's a relief," she said, smiling. "Two days to spare."

Jenny's parents arrived on Wednesday afternoon with Kathy's folks. Cedar Creek began to hum with a life all its own. The rehearsal went off without a hitch, and there was fresh pizza for the rehearsal dinner. The preacher was a pizza lover *and* a horse lover . . . fortunately.

Thursday morning broke clear and crisp, like a perfect apple. Jenny slipped out of bed, dressed quickly, and ran to the barn. She rummaged through her tack trunk to find the bag of silk flowers. She bathed Sunny in the warm water of the wash stall. Then she braided the mare's long mane and tail and rolled each braid around a sponge curler. She did the same to Honey. After draping a wool cooler over each mare to prevent a chill, she was done. "You girls will look lovely," Jenny said, kissing her fingertips like an Italian chef. "I'll see you after breakfast."

She was back in the barn an hour later.

"'Black glitter,'" she read aloud from the label of a bottle. "That will look smart on your hooves." With a hair dryer she fluffed Sunny's curly mane. "A few flowers mixed in and you look like a dream," Jenny said, smiling with satisfaction. "Now, to do the same to Vanessa! No rolling, you girls," she admonished, tossing each one a flake of hay.

In her cottage, Vanessa had rolled her own hair but needed help with painting the nails on her right hand. "You look beautiful, V," Jenny gushed.

"Thank you, thank you for everything," Vanessa said. She smiled almost shyly.

Mr. Perkins led Honey from the barn to the wedding site. Vanessa sat, positively radiant, with a bouquet in one hand. Her dress was cut full so she could sit astride. Her hair was curled in big soft waves, and the flowers in her bouquet matched the ones in the horses' manes. Vanessa's eyes sparkled blue, as blue as the crisp fall sky. Her smile caused everyone who saw her to smile too.

Colton looked smitten the moment Vanessa came into view. Jenny could see the tears welling in his eyes. She had to wipe hers away too. *I wonder if Mom is crying,* she thought. And she was.

"Dearly beloved," the preacher began.

Dearly beloved. That's us. We are His bride, Jenny thought.

Dearly beloved. That's you. That's Vanessa and Colton. All of you here. You are My dearly beloved. Restored.

Chapter Twenty

"Jenn-ee!" Mrs. Thomas yelled, an edge in her voice.

"Yeah, Mom?" Jenny responded lazily.

No answer. Jenny closed her science book and opened her bedroom door. "Where are you?" she called down the stairs.

No answer.

"Mom! Where are you?" Jenny called urgently.

A chair in the kitchen hit the floor with a bang. Jenny flew down the stairs and around the corner. Mrs. Thomas was lying on the floor on her side.

"Mom!" Jenny shrieked, falling to her knees beside her. Their eyes met.

"Phone your dad. It's time!" Mrs. Thomas gasped.

The adrenaline kicked in as Jenny's fingers flew over the buttons. "Dad! It's time," she said into the phone. "You need to get home."

"I'm on my way," he promised.

"Are you all right, Mom?" Jenny breathed, returning to her spot on the floor. The tile was cold and hard. Mrs. Thomas lay still on her side, and then she tensed up.

"Having . . . hard . . . contraction," she panted.

"What can I do?" Jenny begged, setting the phone down.

"Time them."

"OK," Jenny agreed, relieved to be doing something. The contraction ended, and Mrs. Thomas heaved a huge sigh and relaxed. Jenny stared at the clock on the wall. "How are you doing?" she asked.

"Doing fine, sweetie." Mrs. Thomas tried to smile. "But . . . another one is starting."

"Mom, they are two minutes apart!"

"Call 911."

Jenny grabbed the cordless phone and dialed.

"Hello, what is your emergency?" a professional-sounding woman's voice said.

"My mom is in labor and needs help," Jenny cried.

"Is anyone else home with you?"

"No! My dad is coming, but the contractions are two minutes apart, and she's lying on the kitchen floor."

"I'm sending an ambulance right now. You stay on the line with me. My name is Shirley. What's your name, honey?"

"Jenny. Jenny Thomas." Jenny could feel her heartbeat slowing down as she listened to Shirley's calm voice.

"All right, Jenny, do you have any blankets or towels? Something to keep your mom warm?"

Jenny leapt up and ran to the linen closet. She gathered the contents of the second shelf into her arms and returned. *Guest towel, hand towel . . . where are the big towels? Here they are.*

"I've got towels, and a little blanket," she affirmed, placing them over her mother's back.

"You're doing fine," Shirley crooned. "The ambulance should be there soon. How's the mom?"

Jenny rubbed her mother's arm. "Mom, how are you?"

"Hangin' in there. Getting ready for another contraction."

Jenny heard a siren for several relief-filled moments before two EMTs burst through the unlocked front door. Jenny felt pushed aside as frenzied activity took over the small space in the kitchen.

"I'll hang up now," Shirley's voice came through the line. "Jenny . . . are you there?"

"Yes, I'm sorry. I'm just so . . ."

"It's all right. Your mother is in very capable hands. I am hanging up now. You were great."

Jenny placed the phone on the counter and watched a young woman EMT working on her mother.

"OK, now, Mrs. Thomas. We're going to try and get you off this cold floor. Can you move?"

Jenny's mother nodded. She grimaced as she used her arms to push herself onto her back. They almost got the gurney under her.

"Oh . . ." groaned Mrs. Thomas. "This is it!"

"This is what?" cried Mr. Thomas, rushing into the kitchen.

"Dad!" Jenny called. "The baby's coming!"

And that is how Michael Rush Thomas was born on the kitchen floor at 9:30 in the morning on December 20.

Later in the morning, Jenny sat in the corner chair of a hospital room, staring into the eyes of her baby brother. *Wise infant eyes.* "I don't know why we had to come to the hospital," she complained, looking up from the bundle in her arms. "The dangerous part is over."

"I know," Mrs. Thomas agreed. "They wanted to check us both out. We'll be home tomorrow."

"Humph," Jenny snorted, gazing again at the baby. "I want to take him home *now.*"

"Knock, knock," came a familiar male voice from the hallway.

"Colton!" Jenny shrieked.

He waltzed in, hands behind his back. "Judy, Mike, Jenny!" He withdrew a gigantic bouquet of white lilies. "For you, Mrs. Thomas," he said, bowing and smiling. He handed her one of the lilies and then passed the bouquet to Mr. Thomas.

"Why, thank you, kind sir," she said, smiling back. "And pray tell, where is your bride?"

Vanessa's beaming face popped out from around the doorway. "Surprise!" she called. She walked slowly but gracefully, carrying a lovely blue vase for the lilies.

"Judy and Mike. Congratulations!" Vanessa gushed. "And to you too, Jenny."

"Thank you," they chorused.

"Vanessa, have a seat," Jenny insisted, hopping up.

"No, I'm fine," she answered.

"Really, have a seat," Jenny repeated, nodding toward the bundle in her arms.

Vanessa stared at her for a moment and then sat in the vacant chair. She held her arms out stiffly in front of her. "I've never really held a baby, Jen. I'm afraid I'll drop him."

"You'll be fine," Mrs. Thomas assured her.

Jenny carefully placed Michael in Vanessa's waiting arms. Vanessa exhaled as she drew him close. "Oh!" she gasped. "He's so tiny, and . . ." She gazed into the baby's face. "He's looking at me!" Her eyes met Jenny's. "I never wanted to hold a baby. It was such a painful reminder to me. But . . . this . . . this is wonderful."

Restoration.

"Where are you staying?" asked Mr. Thomas.

"Down the street, in a place called Cedar Creek Too," Colton joked. "We know the proprietor."

"Just who is the proprietor of Cedar Creek these days?" Mr. Thomas asked. "Have you found a director for your riding program?"

Vanessa dragged her gaze from Baby Michael's face. "Yes, we think we've found a director. The candidate is still considering our offer."

"Really? Who is it?"

"He's an executive from out of town," Vanessa said in a mysterious tone.

"From the West Coast," Colton added, grinning.

"I know who it is," Jenny said, smiling smugly.

"Who? Tell us!" Mrs. Thomas urged.

Colton winked at Jenny. "Mr. Kevin Perkins."

Jenny's father shook his head. "Talk about a family being brought back together!"

"Restoration!" Jenny crowed. "The years the locusts have eaten are being restored!"

"Amen," Colton agreed.

"It was Honey that convinced my dad," Vanessa said softly. "Jen, you have no idea the healing that old mare has brought. The day I took Daddy to see her, he could not believe his eyes. He tortured himself about Honey for years. I was able to share Jesus with him there in the barn. He said the same thing I said to you. He said, 'Religion is for weaklings.' So I sweetly asked him how things were going without Jesus. Jen, I'll never forget your telling me that it's not about a religion. It's about falling in love with a Man who loves me and my dad so much, He would rather die than live without us. That touched me in a way I cannot describe. And it touched my dad also."

Colton put his big hand on Vanessa's shoulder. "You know, we can always adopt."

Vanessa gazed at him, eyes shining. "I would love to."

Restoration.

Jenny poured the feed for Sunny and Glory. It was relaxing just to watch them eat. She could see the steam rising from their nostrils in the cold morning air. Glory closed her eyes in bliss as she crunched the sweet feed. Soon it would be time to wean the filly. Jenny allowed her mind to wander back over the years, and then forward to what could be.

For I know the plans I have for you.

Thank you, Lord, for loving me, for planning me and all my days.

Get all four books in the Sonrise Farm series!

Based on true stories, Katy Pistole's Sonrise Farm Series about Jenny Thomas and her palomino mare, Sunny, teach children about horses and God's redeeming grace.
US$7.99, Can$11.99 each.

1. *The Palomino*
Jenny Thomas has her heart set on one thing—a golden palomino all her own. Her daring rescue of an abused horse at an auction begins an enduring friendship with Sunny.
0-8163-1863-8. Paperback.

2. *Stolen Gold*
Book two in the series finds Sunny in the clutches of an abusive former owner who wants to collect insurance money on the palomino and her colt. 0-8163-1882-4. Paperback.

3. *Flying High*
A record-breaking jump, Sunny's reputation, and Jenny's relationship with God are all at stake when Jenny and her palomino champion come face to face with their old enemy.
0-8163-1942-1. Paperback.

4. *Morning Glory*
In the most surprising Sonrise Farm adventure yet, Jenny Thomas, Sunny, Mrs. DuBois, Colton the horse trainer, and an old mare named Honey come together in heaven-born circumstances that hurtle them beyond forgiveness to restoration.
0-8163-2036-5. Paperback.

Ride by and get them at your local Adventist Book Center. Call 1-800-765-6955 or get online and shop our virtual store at
<www.AdventistBookCenter.com>
- Read a chapter from your favorite book
- Order online
- Sign up for email notices on new products